Growing in Every Season of Life

A Bible Study for Women

Ruth Ann Larkly

Growing in Every Season of Life
Copyright © 2017 by Ruth Ann Larkly

To place an order or view her other studies, contact Ruth Ann Larkly on Facebook at her Larkly Ladies Bible Study page or email her at ruthann.larkly@gmail.com.
Her books are also available on Amazon.

ISBN (978-0-9859895-3-8)

Printed in USA

Dedication

I dedicate this book to the three persons of God—God the Father, God the Son, and God the Holy Spirit. "For there are three that bear record in heaven, the Father, the Word, and the Holy Ghost: and these three are one" (1 John 5:7).

To my Father—You have listened, talked, rebuked, and encouraged me. I'm thankful You are always there for me!

To Jesus Christ my Savior, the Son—You came to earth to live, die, and live again for me. You know what it is like to live on this earth. Thank You for the spiritual life and victory Your life gives to me!

To the Holy Spirit—You stirred my heart to write this book when I read Psalm 92 in my devotional time. You have strengthened me to write, re-write, and revise (and revise plenty more!). Thank You for Your endless grace to help me keep going and finish Your book.

It is my desire for this Bible study to give You, Lord, all the glory. May it be used to help others spiritually grow so that their life will give You all the glory!

Acknowledgements

Have you ever been asked to do something and agreed, only to discover it took twice as long to finish than you anticipated? That happened to me with this book! Honestly, it would never even be in your hands without the support and encouragement of my friends and family. A great big thank you to everyone the Lord used to help me write and finish this study!

- ❀ Tim Larkly, my husband…seriously, you are the best! You put the book together, designed the cover, read every chapter, listened to my cries, laughed when I laughed—thank you for all you do for me. I am incredibly blessed to have you in my life!

- ❀ Tirzah, Hardy, Acarith, and Selah, my children…I prayed for you at least ten years before the Lord gave you to me. I have given you back to Him, and I hope with all my heart that you will love Him and grow in every season of your life!

- ❀ Sandy Wilhelm, the best mom I could ever have…in my younger school days I would wish you only used your proofreading skills at the office and not on my school papers; now I value your sharp eagle eye. Thank you for your countless enthusiasm and thorough markings with every chapter!

- ❀ Alice Klies, president of my writing club and friend…I will always be grateful for that first personal meeting we had at Jerona Café when you gave me your valuable critique on my chapters. I know my writing still has plenty of room for improvement, but thank you for helping me to learn and grow in the craft of writing!

- ❀ Mary Rice…as we hiked the Grand Canyon, you listened to me talk about my ideas for my very first Bible study and encouraged me to go for it. Thank you for your friendship and support you continue to give to me!

- Sue Smith, my godly, grandma friend…thank you for the suggestions and valuable input you gave for the chapter to the grandmas!
- Whitney Beam, my (then) newlywed friend…thank you for reading the chapter for wives and your wise feedback!
- Hannah Furse, my young lady friend…thank you for your approval and enthusiasm of the chapter for young ladies!
- Chrissy Dedmon…thank you for reading every chapter, sending me encouraging messages, and writing a book review!
- Renee Warneke…thank you for inspiring me to set up a Facebook account for my Bible studies, reading the chapters, writing a review, and supporting me!
- Deana Royalty…thank you for your words of encouragement. I still remember the first card you sent me after my first Bible study came out. Your words with this Bible study have continued to encourage me!
- Jaime Bunton…your love for the Lord and life were a huge part in my growing-up years. I will always be grateful for our friendship!
- Natalie Walker…the Lord sent you to be my friend during a crucial time of my life. Thank you for being there for me and helping me grow more in the Lord!
- Laurie Jones…we were young ladies together, newlyweds, and mothers. As we go through our physical and spiritual seasons, thank you for helping me to grow during them!

Table of Contents

Introduction

My first memory of hearing the phrase *seasons of life* makes me smile. About 17 years ago, when I was single, I sat in a ladies' Sunday school class and heard my pastor's wife and other ladies discuss the various *seasons of life*. As my friends shared with the class their tidbits of wisdom, I understood what they talked about, but, honestly, I don't think I really understood everything they talked about (if that makes sense!). My friends knew I wanted to be married with a family of my own and would encourage me to enjoy my single season of life.

Guess what advice people give me now, even complete strangers, when I'm out with my kids? They say, "Enjoy your time with your kids. They grow up way too fast." I have also said the same thing to mothers with small children. Why do we encourage others to enjoy their seasons of life? It's because the longer we live, the more we realize life is a gift. Life is short. Seasons come and seasons go. People change. We change.

Don't you love how God designed the earthly seasons? My top three favorites are spring, summer, and fall. (Winter's not on the list because of the cold!) I'm so thankful the Lord created each season. Just imagine how dreary everything would be if it always stayed the same! God's earthly seasons have such purpose, change, and beauty—and the same applies to our spiritual seasons of life. And like the earthly seasons have growth, God wants us to grow in our spiritual seasons of life.

A couple years ago, when I was going through a hard spiritual season of life, I read through Psalm 92 in my morning devotions. Three verses really caught my attention: "The righteous shall flourish like the palm tree: he shall grow like a cedar in Lebanon. Those that be planted in the house of the LORD shall flourish in the courts of our God. They shall still bring forth fruit in old age; they shall be fat and flourishing" (Ps. 92:12-14).

It took me a moment, but I realized these verses beautifully show me that I should grow in every season of life—through the end of my life. Just because I had been experiencing a harder season didn't mean I could just give the Lord a "Get out of Growth Free" pass to Him. God wants me to grow in every season of life—not because of me and my circumstances—but because of Him and all that He has done for me. And that is how this Bible study was born!

If you have read my other Bible studies, you know I'm passionate to study the lives of women from the Bible. This Bible study continues that passion. It talks about women from the Bible, their seasons of life, and how we can grow from their life. Six chapters of this study can be applied to all women, and four chapters are written specifically to women who are young ladies, wives, mothers, and grandmothers. Even if you're not in any of these seasons, I would like to encourage you to read through the chapters; there are biblical truths that can still be a help to you. Grandma Lois' life and chapter really spoke to my heart—even though I am a little far off from being a grandma!

I do hope you enjoy your seasons of life. I also hope you enjoy my Bible study on the seasons of life. However, more than enjoying your seasons of life—I really hope you grow in every season of life!

Happy Growing! Love, Ruth Ann

Chapter One

Growing to Bring Forth Fruit

In our Younger through Our Older Seasons of Life

Phoebe and Dorcas

A few years ago, Tim and I walked by our neighbor Justin's house and admired his beautiful grape vines. Justin, a horticulturist who taught at our local junior college, came over to say hello, and within ten minutes Tim decided we should grow our own grapes too. Justin was a great help to get us started; he brought over some cuttings from some of his older branches and helped Tim set them up along our fence. Together they dug holes and fertilized them; as they worked, Justin would explain to Tim how to take care of them. For the first few months, everyone in the family loved to water and look after the needs of the grapevines. Everything went great until—we left for summer vacation! Uh-oh! We forgot to ask our neighbors to water and take care of the grapes! By the time we came back, the Arizona sun had scorched the vines and branches. Our whole family felt disappointed to know we wouldn't get any homegrown grapes from them.

I'm so thankful our heavenly Father never forgets about us! Once we receive Jesus into our life, we belong in His spiritual vineyard and the Father gives us tender loving care. As we grow in the Lord, the Lord desires for us to bring forth good fruit. Did you know that the Lord wants you, from your younger seasons up through your older seasons, to bring forth good fruit?

Do you wonder how your life can bring forth good fruit? Two women whose lives produced good fruit are Phoebe and Dorcas. Phoebe's spiritual fruit caught the eye of Paul, who trusted her to carry a book he wrote to the Christians in Rome. Dorcas used her needle making skills for widows. In their own unique way, each woman brought forth good fruit and used it to give glory to the Lord!

Our Fruit Comes from our Relationship with the Lord
Phoebe—Romans 16:1-2

Phoebe lived in the city of Cenchrea, a village on the southeastern tip of modern day Greece. About eight miles south of Corinth and a port for the city of Corinth's ships, Paul and other believers planted a church in Cenchrea. A Gentile woman, Phoebe accepted Jesus as her Savior and attended the church. Her name means "bright or shining" from the Greek goddess of the moon, and Phoebe radiated light to others in the spiritually dark region of Corinth.

Phoebe served with Paul in her church and learned of his desire to travel and meet with the Christians at Rome. Paul wanted to go to Rome (Rom. 1:13), yet up to this time in his life God had other plans for Paul. He decided to write the Christians a letter and, since he knew he could trust Phoebe, he asked her to deliver his book of Romans to the Christians at Rome.

Humbled to know Paul entrusted her with his beloved letter, Phoebe agreed to go on the mission. "It was risky for him to become so dependent on another person...With Phoebe, however, Paul...knew that she had a good reputation and would represent him. She had proved that she had a heart for God and His service."[1] Because Paul knew the Christians at Rome would be cautious to welcome a newcomer into their fellowship, Paul included in his letter a recommendation for the church to welcome Phoebe (Rom. 16:1).

Phoebe clung with all her might to the scroll as she walked to Macedonia (Greece) and rode in a creaky ship to southeastern Italy.

10

Once there, she traveled on the Appian Way, one of the first important highways the Roman army built in 312 BC.[2] She had to be careful; a single woman traveling in the year AD 57 attracted plenty of attention. Heading north, a tired but happy Phoebe paced herself on the journey. How relieved and excited she felt when she arrived in Rome to give Paul's beloved letter to the Christians!

Phoebe's willingness to risk her life for Paul and the Lord shows her spiritual fruit. Fruit comes from what we are like on the inside that pops up on the outside. Good spiritual fruit doesn't just happen—it comes from our relationship with the Lord. To help us understand our spiritual relationship with the Lord and how we bear fruit, Jesus gives us a picture in John 15:1-10:

- ❧ Jesus is the True Vine. An earthly vine is the "trunk" of the plant that grows out of the ground. The vine ends in a large gnarl from which branches spread across on either side of a trellis.
- ❧ God the Father is the husbandman (or in today's language, a vinedresser). He gives the branches on the vine tender care. He positions and prunes the branches in a special way so that they can grow off either side of the vine and give off fruit.
- ❧ Christians are the branches that grow on either side where the vine ends in a large gnarl. Any fruit we yield comes from our connection with Jesus and the care of our Father. Our relationship with Jesus and the Father is intimate, full of love and trust.

When we have a relationship with the Lord, we will bear fruit. Actually, we can bring forth lots of good fruit! Because our fruit comes from our relationship with the Lord, our connection to the Lord determines the amount of fruit we yield. Jesus tells us to be "clean" and to "abide" in Him (Jn. 15:3-4). Like any relationship, what we put into our relationship with the Lord will determine what we get out of our relationship. Want to be fruitful? Keep abiding with the Lord!

We are Known by our Fruit

Phoebe received a warm welcome from the Christians at Rome. The Christians in Rome were "possibly some who were converted on the day of Pentecost (Acts 2:10)...or it may be that converts of Paul or of other apostles founded the church there."[3] Can you picture their excitement to receive a letter from Paul and gather around to read it? Phoebe knew every moment of risk on her mission had been worth it.

When the Christians got to the last chapter of Romans, Phoebe heard Paul mention her name in the first verse. He wrote a glowing, 53 word report about her! It began, "I [Paul] commend unto you Phebe our sister, which is a servant of the church which is at Cenchrea" (Rom. 16:1).

The word *servant* and the word *deacon* come from the Greek word *diakonos*. Because of this, some believe Phoebe had an official title of a deacon. However, *diakonos* is neither a male or female word, and women were not to teach or usurp authority over a man (1 Tim. 2:12). This doesn't minimize Phoebe's role at her church. She did have a very important ministry—the serving ministry. "If hers was not an official ministry, it was certainly a most gracious and effective one."[4]

Paul continued, "That ye receive her in the Lord, as becometh saints, and that ye assist her in whatsoever business she hath need of you: for she hath been a succourer of many, and of myself also" (Rom. 16:2). During this time, Rome's population neared around one million people.[5] What a blessing for Phoebe to know the Roman Christians would help her navigate her way around the big city to conduct her business transactions.

A "succourer of many" meant she helped people during their time of need. Paul used the Greek word *prostastis* which means a patron, a wealthy person in the Jewish community who financially helped someone else. It's highly possible that Phoebe used her own personal finances to support Paul and others.[6] Phoebe was known as a giver, and her spiritual good fruit were seen by all who knew her.

Jesus tells us in Matthew 7:16 that we will know other people "by their fruits." This also means other people know us by our fruits. What we do on the outside shows people what we are like on the inside. Yes, we can sometimes put on a good show with our good works and look good on the outside. However, this cheap, imitation fruit won't last; only real spiritual fruit will remain. Jesus told us to "go and bring forth fruit, and that your fruit should remain" (Jn. 15:16).

Good works are a product of our relationship with the Lord, but our spiritual fruit involves more than what we do. It comes from deep within us—to our spirit and our heart. Yes, Phoebe did good works; but her spirit and heart for the Lord showed her spiritual fruit. Good works that come from a good heart give us good fruit.

From our younger seasons through our older seasons, here are some ways a Christian woman produces spiritual fruit:
- She develops Christian character (Gal. 5:22-23)
- She lives a life that pleases the Lord with good works (Col. 1:10)
- She sees people come to the Lord from her life (Rom. 1:13)
- She praises and thanks the Lord (Heb. 13:15)
- She adds to her faith and knowledge of the Lord (2 Pet. 1:5-8)

Wow! There are so many ways we can bring forth good fruit and have it remain! Do others see good fruit in your life? Let's use our fruit for others to know the Lord!

Our Fruit Needs a Good Pruning for it to Grow
Dorcas—Acts 9:36-42

Dorcas lived in a seaport called Joppa. Joppa was the port in which King Solomon ordered wood and materials for the temple to be shipped, and where Jonah the prophet boarded a ship to run away from God. "Now there was at Joppa a certain disciple named Tabitha, which by interpretation is called Dorcas" (Acts 9:36).

A disciple of Jesus, Dorcas did more than just believe—she followed the Lord with her whole heart. She gave so much of herself to others that she was known to be "full of good works and almsdeeds which she did" (Acts 9:36). ("The word "did" is in the imperfect tense which means she habitually practiced doing good works."[7])

Dorcas knew that widow were "generally the most apt to be neglected or oppressed"[8] and decided to help them. With her gift from the Lord that involved the use of a needle, Dorcas began a sewing ministry for the widows. She happily stitched beautiful garments and gave them to anyone who needed them. It's possible she "must have been a woman of means to serve humanity as freely as she did."[9]

Dorcas ministered to many widows until she became very sick. Maybe as she lay on her sickbed she continued to work and finish her clothing projects. Did she wonder why God would allow her to have health issues while she tried to help the widows? Dorcas had no idea how God would use her sickness, and ultimately her death, to bring forth more good spiritual fruit from her life!

Let's look at how a vinedresser prunes His branches in order to bring forth fruit. To get the maximum amount of fruit from a branch, the vinedresser prunes, or cuts off, the "shoots" that grow on the branches because they weigh down and weaken the branches. He whittles and cuts away on each branch to strengthen them. Even

14

branches that have fruit he will cut out for the branch to bring forth more good fruit. The vinedresser's goal is for each branch to produce more and more good fruit.

In our spiritual life, God the Father cuts off of our lives those things that limit our fruitfulness or prevent us from bringing forth more good fruit. Jesus tells us God's role in our life as a Husbandman in John 15:2. "And every branch that beareth fruit, he purgeth it, that it may bring forth more fruit." In the Greek, the word *purgeth* literally means "to prune, or to cleanse."

More than bringing forth fruit, we should want our lives to bring forth *more* fruit. This means we'll need to embrace our Father's pruning and cleansing in our life. Yes, spiritual pruning can be a painful process. Whether it's a sickness, a kind of loss, struggle, or trial, with tender loving care God takes his pruning knife and cuts out those things that weigh us down and weaken our spiritual life. We may not understand why God does everything He does, but one thing's for sure—we can be comforted to know that after God prunes us, we can bring forth more fruit!

Our Good Fruit will Bring Glory to the Lord

Dorcas' sickness took a turn for the worse and then she died. Her friends mourned her death, washed her dead body, and placed it in an upper chamber. Their refusal to bury her shows their hope for a miracle. When they heard the apostle Peter stayed in Lydda, a town about 11 miles away,[10] "they sent unto him two men, desiring him that he would not delay to come to them" (Acts 9:38).

Once in Joppa, Peter headed straight to the upper room to view her body. "And all the widows stood by him weeping, and shewing the coats and garments which Dorcas made, while she was with them" (Acts 9:39). Peter quickly instructed the broken hearted women to leave the room. Alone with Dorcas, he knelt down and prayed for her. "And turning him to the body said, Tabitha, arise" (Acts 9:40).

Dorcas opened her eyes, saw Peter, and sat up! She grasped his outstretched hands while he lifted her up from the bed. Can you imagine her trying to understand everything that just happened while he called out to her friends that she was alive? And then, to everyone's wide-eyed amazement, "Peter presented her alive" (Acts 9:41).

Word of the miracle spread in Joppa faster than the ships sailed in the harbor! "Hey, did you hear the amazing miracle Peter performed on Dorcas? He brought her dead body back to life! She lives! Her God must be the true God." "And it was known throughout all Joppa; and many believed in the Lord" (Acts 9:42). Dorcas' testimony brought an amazing spiritual revival to her town; her good fruit gave the Lord all the glory!

This is why we should want to bring forth good fruit—so our life can glorify the Lord. Jesus said, "Herein is my Father glorified, that ye bear much fruit" (Jn. 15:8). All the pain in the pruning and abiding in the Lord will all be worth it when our life brings glory to the Lord! Can our purpose for life get any better than that?

Imagine you walk by a beautiful vineyard. You notice the vinedresser working hard in the field. The vines are green and lush. Large clusters of grapes and big leaves lightly hang on the branches. Now, would you think, "Wow, he sure was lucky to have all that fruit magically appear."? Probably not. You would know the fruit came as a result of his days and years spent to take care of his vineyard. Maybe you would sample his fruit to confirm your suspicions—this man knows how to grow grapes!

That's what happens when we bear fruit—we make our Father look good. Our fruit brings Him glory when others look at our life and see how good He is. Others want to draw near to Him—not because of what we have done—but because of all they see Him do in our life.

Do people see fruit in your life? Does your good fruit make the Lord look good and give Him glory?

Phoebe's and Dorcas' Roots and Fruits

Since Paul didn't arrive in Rome until three years later after Phoebe, it's a good thing he trusted Phoebe to deliver "that book, that most important perhaps of all books in terms of its presentation of the gospel."[11] From the early Christians of Rome to the Christians of today, we have benefited from the spiritual fruit of Phoebe's life. Her fruit has pointed many people to the Lord and brought so much glory to the Lord.

Dorcas' testimony made such a spiritual impact on people that even today, two thousand years later, there are Dorcas societies' established around the world to make clothes for the needy. Though Dorcas' needle "embroidered her name into the world,"[12] her spiritual fruit also made God's name known. I wonder, since she lived in the seaport of Joppa, how far the sailor's stories spread about her miracle from the Lord. Back then and even now, her spiritual fruit brings people to the Lord and gives Him glory.

How can you grow in bringing forth good fruit in your younger to your older seasons of life?

To grow in bringing forth good fruit, make sure you keep growing from your younger to your older seasons of life. By the time you reach the end of your life, the Father will be able to collect big clusters of spiritual fruit from off your branches. Throughout your lifetime, keep abiding with the Lord. Stay connected to Him. Allow and embrace the Father's pruning of anything that may hinder your spiritual growth. "We have to trust and obey... detach ourselves from all else… reach out after Him… cling to Him… sink ourselves into Him — except we abide, we cannot bear fruit."[13]

Digging Deeper

Memorize John 15:16: *"Ye have not chosen me, but I have chosen you, and ordained you, that ye should go and bring forth fruit, and that your fruit should remain."*

Branching Out

1. Philippians 1:11 says we Christians are to be filled with "fruits of righteousness." Why? _____
   _____

2. Since we are known by our fruit, would your friends and family say you yield good or bad fruit? Why? _____
   _____

3. What are some areas in your life that you need to have cut out so that you can grow more to bring forth fruit? _____
   _____

4. In Psalm 92:14-15, when we bring forth fruit what does our life really show?_____
   _____

I can grow and bring forth fruit in my younger season to my older season

by _____

_____

_____

Chapter Two

Growing Stronger in Your Christian Beliefs

Season: Young Lady

A Little Maid
2 Kings 5:1

I worked my first job at a Golden Corral in my senior year of high school. Never before had I faced the challenge and opportunity to work and be around so many unsaved people. I arrived at work after school in my Christian school uniform and made my Christian beliefs no secret to my coworkers. My friendly ways finally paid off when several coworkers would open up and share their life story with me. During these times they would ask me tough, spiritual questions. Some searched for honest answers while others, bitter and skeptical, would challenge my beliefs.

All their questions caused me to do some deep soul searching. I understood the man who cried to Jesus, "Lord, I believe; help thou mine unbelief" (Mark 9:24). I made a notebook with Bible verses, passages, and thoughts to help me. My pastor let me borrow some of his books; one in particular, called "Kingdom of the Cults," helped me understand other religions and my own doctrinal beliefs. I never led anyone to the Lord that year, but I learned and grew so much in my spiritual life. My beliefs became very important to me, and I discovered how they affected not only my life but also the lives of many others around me.

The Lord wants us to believe in Him, and then He gives power to those who do. "That the God of our Lord Jesus Christ…may give unto you the spirit of wisdom and revelation in the knowledge of him…And what is the *exceeding greatness of his power to us-ward who believe*, according to the working of his mighty power" (Eph. 1:19) (emphasis mine). What you believe will affect your entire life. Your beliefs affect where29 your spend eternity after you die, how you live on earth, who and what kind of man you marry, how you raise your children, what you do for the Lord, and the kind of legacy you leave behind.

A young lady the Bible calls "a little maid" knew what she believed. In a time of personal trials and struggles, her beliefs strengthened her during the rough times. They also influenced a general, his family, and friends from a heathen country to believe in the Lord!

Do you know how to grow stronger in your beliefs?

The Little Maid and her family lived in the northern part of Israel that bordered Syria. Reports of Syrian army victories under a general named Naaman made their way to the Little Maid and her people (2 Kings 5:1). Under direct orders of the Syrian king, General Naaman began to raid the Israelite towns by the Syrian border. On one of these raids, he kidnapped the Little Maid. Did she ever know what happened to her family?

Naaman assigned the Little Maid to be a maid for his wife (who I call Mrs. Naaman). Despite feeling sad and homesick, the Little Maid faithfully served Mrs. Naaman. The Naaman family had wealth and status, and the Little Maid discovered they also had a family secret—Naaman had a life-threatening disease called leprosy.

The Little Maid sympathized with Naaman and said to Mrs. Naaman: "Would God my lord were with the prophet [Elisha] that is in Samaria! for he would recover him of his leprosy" (2 Kings

5:3). "'Would God,' emphasizes the earnestness of her testimony…It was filled with great compassion and concern."[14]

Honestly, I don't know about you, but if someone ever kidnapped me, and I discovered my kidnapper had a deadly disease, I would be thrilled! I certainly wouldn't want him to find a cure either! This Little Maid amazes me; even in her discouraging circumstances she fully believed in the power of her Lord. She could have switched or hid her beliefs when she arrived in Syria, but she didn't. Her strong faith in the Lord helped her be strong in her beliefs.

In 2015, a Christian article said 70% of teenagers involved in church youth groups quit attending church when they become adults.[15] How sad! The teens claimed they no longer believed in God, but I wonder how real their beliefs in the Lord became to them in the first place. Are your beliefs real to you?

Do you want to grow stronger in your Christian beliefs? God's Word will strengthen your faith. Faith means you take God at His Word, and happens when you know His Word. Romans 10:17 says, "Faith cometh by hearing, and hearing by the Word of God." What you listen to will affect your faith. Be very careful to listen to people who challenge the Bible and your faith. If their questions bring you to the Bible, you can grow stronger in your faith; if their questions cause you to withdraw from the Bible, your faith will weaken. Your Christian journey began by faith and needs to continue in faith through God's Word.

Do you read your Bible every day? It's good if you read it on occasion, but greater if you can make it an everyday habit. As a young girl, I read my Bible with my family every day until I went to Bible college. It became a struggle to read on my own with no mom or dad to say, "Get your Bible; it's time for family devotions." Through my years on my own, I struggled to be consistent.

However, I didn't give up trying. I eventually made it a habit to spend every morning with the Lord before my day began—a habit I enjoy doing. My advice to help you get started would be to find a time that works for you every day, stick to it every day, and ask someone to keep you accountable for every day. Make it an enjoyable time for you. The more you like doing a habit, the more successful you will be to keep it. As you make this to be a habit, it will strengthen and guide you in your upcoming seasons of life.

A couple years ago, while out door knocking in Cottonwood, I met a sweet teenager named JoJo. JoJo told me she did believe in the Bible and agreed to listen to me explain from the Bible how to go to heaven. I showed her verses on the plan of salvation and presented to her the gospel story. She asked questions, answered questions, and made comments throughout our entire conversation. I really thought she wanted to be saved. Then she said, "Well, can I tell you what I believe?" I said sure. She told me how a few years earlier she had a vision that when she died, she would became a goddess of the stars (and I honestly can't remember the other bizarre stuff she said after that). Then she told me that maybe one day she would "try out Christianity!"

I'm so thankful my beliefs come from the Bible and not something I dream up. I'm so thankful to have a personal relationship with the Lord and no desire to "try out" other religions. Aren't we so blessed to have the Bible? Let's keep reading God's Word so we can strengthen our faith and grow stronger in our beliefs!

Do you speak what you believe?

Mrs. Naaman perceived the Little Maid's compassion to be sincere for her husband, and she told Naaman about their conversation. Naaman relayed the information to his boss, the king (who also wanted his star general to be healed). The king of Syria said, "Go to, go, and I will send a letter unto the king of Israel. And he departed, and took with him ten talents of silver, and six thousand pieces of gold, and ten changes of raiment" (2 Kings 5:4-5). The value of everything the king gave Naaman is estimated to be around 4 million dollars![16]

Naaman journeyed south to see Jehoram, the king of Israel, and appeared before him with his letter. When Jehoram read the letter from the king of Sryia, he acted strange and said, "Am I God, to kill and to make alive, that this man doth send unto me to recover a man of his leprosy? Wherefore consider, I pray you, and see how he seeketh a quarrel against me" (2 Kings 5:7).

Naaman felt confused; he didn' intend to pick a fight with the king. When the prophet Elisha heard about Naaman, he messaged the king to send Naaman to his house. I'm sure by this time Naaman hoped his Little Maid knew what she was talking about! His entire life depended on what she said and believed!

Do you know what you believe? No worries if you don't have all the answers to every deep theological issue. However, do you have a general knowledge of the Bible basics? Once you know what you believe, you will be able to speak up about your beliefs. Second Corinthians 4:13 says, "We having the same spirit of faith, according as it is written, I believed, and therefore have I spoken; we also believe, and therefore speak."

Here are some scenarios to show you why it's important to know what you believe—

🕊 You told your boss when he hired you that you won't work on Sundays. But when you looked at your work schedule, you noticed he put you down to work on Sunday from 8am to 4pm. What do you believe about working on Sundays? What would you say?

_____

_____

🌸 A nice, handsome guy from your college and career asks you out to dinner. You know he's a Christian. What do you believe about dating? What would you say?

_____

_____

🌸 You live on your own. No longer do your parents have a say in the type of clothes you wear, the music you listen to, the type of church you attend, and the friends you make. Do you know what you believe about these topics?

_____

_____

Have you ever seen "Watters World" from Fox news? Occasionally I'll watch a few online clips when I scope out the news. A guy named Jesse Watters hits the streets and asks people what they believe concerning various issues. Some people have no idea what they believe while others have the craziest answers for what they think. It's time for you to be ready—people will come to you with questions. Some will be in search of earnest answers while others might just want to debate you. Now's the time to know what you believe, and when you do—speak what you be believe!

Do your beliefs affect others to know the Lord?

Let's imagine the rest of the Little Maid's story when Naaman came home. Surely the household buzzed with excitement at his arrival and gasped when they saw him show off his clear, smooth skin. What a miracle! Naaman couldn't wait to share with everyone his story of God's healing.

Naaman: "Blessed be the Lord for healing me from my leprosy! God's power and His prophet Elisha performs miracles like the Little Maid said. At first I was angry with the prophet Elisha. When I arrived at his house, he didn't even greet me, a powerful general! My servants and I waited outside his front door in my prize horses and chariot until Elisha's servant gave me a message to wash seven times in the Jordan River."

"'Behold, I thought, He will surely come out to me, and stand, and call on the name of the LORD his God, and strike his hand over the place, and recover the leper [a typical action "of those engaged in magical arts"[17]]. Are not Abana and Pharpar, rivers of Damascus, better than all the waters of Israel? may I not wash in them, and be clean?' (2 Kings 5:11-12). I stormed away in a rage until my servants reasoned with me to do what Elisha said."

"When I stepped in the muddy Jordan River, I wondered how it could heal me. However, I chose to obey the prophet's message and dipped in it seven times. On the seventh time I came up out of the water, the miracle happened—my leprosy disappeared! My skin hasn't been this smooth since I was a child! Immediately I went to thank Elisha. I know it would have been easier and closer for me to come straight home (the trip cost him an extra 50 miles[18]), but I wanted to meet and thank him."

Wow—the Little Maid's beliefs affected Naaman to become healed and a true believer! Isn't it amazing how one life can affect someone else's life and eternity? One of the greatest joys in your Christian life will be for others to know and grow in the Lord from your life (1 Thess. 2:20). Your life—

🌿 Reveals the kind of Christian you are (1 Thess. 1:5). Did you know that people watch you to see if you live what you believe?

🌿 Influences people to follow Jesus and follow you (1 Thess. 1:6). Do people see Jesus in you?

🌸 Becomes an example to strengthen other believers. Did you know that the people you influence can then influence other people for the Lord (1 Thess. 1:7-8)?

Has someone ever believed in the Lord because of your Christian influence? Have you ever led someone else to pray and accept Jesus to be their Savior? These will be exciting spiritual moments for you. You may think, "I'm just a young lady. My life can't make that much of a difference in someone else's." Oh, yes it can! The Little Maid's life influenced a stubborn general to be saved, and God can use your life to influence Him for others too!

Do you live what you believe?

The Little Maid listened to Naaman continue his story: "When I returned and stood before Elisha, I told him, 'Behold, now I know that there is no God in all the earth, but in Israel: now therefore, I pray thee, take a blessing of thy servant' (2 Kings 5:15). I tried to offer him my gifts, but he refused. He said, 'As the LORD liveth, before whom I stand, I will receive none' (2 Kings 5:16). I knew then he wanted nothing for himself; he only wanted me to know God's power."

"Did you know I even brought back fresh dirt from Israel? I asked Elisha if I could take some from his land to bring back home with me. I wanted dirt from Israel to build an altar to God." Wow! Naaman didn't plan to keep his new faith a secret; he wanted to build an altar at his house for all to see.

"One question I did ask Elisha. Since I take the Syrian king to worship his false god at the house of Rimmon (an idol temple), I allow the king to lean on my arms and help him bow. Elisha granted me both pardon and peace in the matter. We then headed home. Thank you, Little Maid, for living what you believed; your life brought me to know the true Lord."

26

Can you see Naaman, too, decided to live what he believed? His new beliefs changed his life and how he would live his life! "When a person is converted, his attitudes change; his convictions change. He sees right and wrong far differently than before his conversion."[19]

Romans 6:8 says, "Now if we be dead with Christ, *we believe that we shall also live with him*" (emphasis mine). More than eternal life, this talks about how we should live here on earth. Are you living a changed life? If you believe—

- ❀ The Bible, you will read it.
- ❀ Jesus died to save you from your sins, you will love and follow Him.
- ❀ You are to obey your parents, you will honor them.
- ❀ Baptism is the first step in obedience to Christ, you will be baptized.
- ❀ Heaven and Hell are real, you will share with others the good news about eternal salvation through Jesus Christ.
- ❀ God lives inside you, you will abstain from smoking, drugs, sexual impurities, and alcohol abuse.
- ❀ God's timing and will to be best for who you marry, you will wait and keep yourself pure for him.

Yes, people may make fun of you for what you believe and how you live. But can I tell you a secret? Don't let their carefree ways fool you; some of the most miserable people I know are Christians who don't live for the Lord or the unsaved in a desperate search for peace. Your beliefs affect how you live, and how you live will affect others to know the Lord. May the Lord help you grow stronger in Him for others to know Him!

The Little Maid's Roots and Fruits

Even though the Little Maid's kidnappers took her to a different country, there was something they couldn't take away from her— her beliefs! In Israel, she attended the temple and worshipped God; in Syria, she continued to believe in the Lord and live for Him. God used her life to bring healing, peace, and joy to others. Her life shined as a light in the darkness of Syria and effected Naaman, and probably his family, to believe in the Lord.

How can you grow in your beliefs as a young lady?

The Lord gives you support and tools to help you on your Christian journey—your family, friends, Bible, church group and leader. Use what He gives and places in your path to help grow in Him. However, only you through the Lord's help can form good spiritual habits; only you by God's grace can do your spiritual growing. "Sow a thought and you reap an action; sow an act and you reap a habit; sow a habit and you reap a character; sow a character and you reap a destiny."[20] Now's the time for you to sow good spiritual seeds to help you grow in the Lord!

Digging Deeper

Memorize Ephesians 1:19: *"And what is the exceeding greatness of his power to us-ward who believe, according to the working of his mighty power."*

Branching Out

1. From Second Peter 4:13, what should we be ready to do?

_____

_____

2. Do you live what you believe in the types of clothing you wear, music you listen to, church you attend, and in your Bible reading?_____

   _____

   _____

3. How can what you believe have a positive effect on others around you? _____

   _____

   _____

4. Check the box below that applies to you.

   ☐ I don't spend any quiet time with the Lord but through His help I will start this week.

   —OR—

   ☐ I read my Bible but not every day. I commit to spending quiet time with the Lord every day this week

   —OR—

   ☐ I commit to spending quiet time with the Lord for one whole year.

I can grow and bear fruit as a young lady by_____

_____

_____

Chapter Three

Growing in Boldness to our Father

Season of Health Issues

A Bleeding Woman
Matthew 9:20-22

I saw my husband Tim's boldness during the second occasion we officially met. My matchmaker grandparents had worked hard for two years to get us together; they were excited that my family and I would attend Sunday morning services at their church that Tim pastored. Tim accepted their lunch invitation and my whole family and I enjoyed getting to know him (especially me!). Later that night, after the church's evening service, I walked around and visited with the church people. I noticed Tim out of the corner of my eye watch me. I smiled back and he continued to stare at me! He gave me an "I'm interested in you look." I blushed and looked away; I thought, "This guy is bold!" When we officially were dating later, I brought up the fun memory. He told me he stared at me for a reason—to send me a signal that he was interested in me. Well, it worked!

Having boldness in the Lord means we approach Him with passion and confidence. The purpose of our boldness draws us closer to Him. Our boldness comes from a comfort in God's presence and an assurance that He hears our prayers; there's no hesitation or fear when we go to the Lord. We can be bold in our access to the Lord, speech, and actions because of our relationship with Him. Ephesians 3:12 says that through the Lord "we have boldness and access with confidence by the faith of him."

Did you know that we need to have boldness in a season of health issues? The Bleeding Woman's boldness will amaze and touch your heart. By faith, her boldness in Jesus drew her closer to the Lord. In return, He gave her bold promises back!

Boldness by our Faith

The Bleeding Woman overheard amazing true stories of miracles Jesus performed. The more she heard, the more determined she became to meet Jesus. Her heart's desire was for Him to heal her of a disease that handicapped and embarrassed her for 12 years—she bled all the time. The Bible says she "was diseased with an issue of blood" (Matt. 9:20). The phrase *issue of blood* means a hemorrhage, which indicated she would discharge large amounts of blood all the time.

Bleeding once a month is bad enough; can you imagine her level of pain for 12 straight years? She had no modern day hygiene, no ibuprofen, no heating pads, and no chocolate (!). Mark 5:26 says she "had suffered many things [treatments] of many physicians, and had spent all that she had, and was nothing bettered, but rather grew worse."

A lengthy prescription found in the Talmud for medical treatment of her disease gives us some idea of what she probably went through. "Take the gum of Alexandria, the weight of a zuzee (a fractional silver coin); of alum, the same; of crocus, the same. Let them be bruised together, and given in wine to the woman that has an issue of blood. If this does not benefit [her], take Persian onions three logs (pints); boil them in wine, and give her to drink, and say, 'Arise from thy flux [heavy flow of blood].' If this does not cure her, set her in a place where two ways meet, and let her hold a cup of wine in her right hand, and let someone come behind and frighten her, and say, 'Arise from thy flux.' But if that do no good, take a

31

handful of cumin (a kind of fennel), a handful of crocus, and a handful of fenugreek (another kind of fennel). Let these be boiled in wine and give them her to drink, and say, 'Arise from thy flux!'"[21]

And then if that didn't work…"Let them dig seven ditches, in which let them burn some cuttings of vines, not four years old. Let her take in her hand a cup of wine, and let them lead her away from this ditch, and make her sit down over that. And let them remove her from that, and make her sit down over another, saying to her at each remove, 'Arise from thy flux!'"[22]

Can you imagine her embarrassment to find someone to scare her or, and I'm not trying to be crude, her weariness to crouch over and bleed into a pit? She lost all hope in the natural remedies and doctor's prescriptions. In fact, the doctors made her worse, not better! She came to a realization—her only hope could be in the Lord, not man.

When Jesus arrived back in town, the Bleeding Woman headed to meet Him. To her dismay, she discovered lots of other people wanted to see Jesus. A large crowd followed Jesus, led by a rabbi named Jairus who wanted Jesus to heal his dying daughter. The Bleeding Woman joined the pack and, though frail and weak, weaved her way through and around the crowd. She determined to not let her health issues keep her from Jesus. Her faith in Jesus gave her the boldness she needed to make her way to Him.

Maybe you can relate. You have struggled with health issues and been in and out of the doctor's office. Maybe you also need to come to the realization, if you haven't already, that your faith can't be in people; it needs to be in the Lord. When we have faith in the Lord, we can have boldness and go to Him with all our needs. "The confidence of being welcomed and accepted when we go into God's presence springs from our faith in him."[23]

Again, Ephesians 3:12 says, "In whom we have boldness and access with confidence by the faith of him." Faith gives us confidence in the Lord; faith strengthens our relationship with Him. The more our faith grows, the more we will go to the Lord.

When our daughter Selah wore her corrective helmet, I had zero faith in her specialist; I had to place all my faith in the Lord. When our specialist commented how he wished other families were faithful to make their kids wear their helmets, I told him, "It's by faith; every time I put that helmet on her head it's an act of faith."

Do you want to have boldness when you go the Lord? You first need to have faith. If you don't believe the Lord to be who He says, then you will falter on your way to Him. If you believe the Lord to be all He says to be, then nothing will stop you to have boldness. Your faith combined with boldness won't let anything keep you from going to Him. Do everything you can to draw closer to Him!

Boldness in our Access

Joining the massive crowd took a big step for this woman who lived a private life. The Bleeding Woman hoped with all her heart to not see anyone she knew. Her disease made her a social disgrace to society; she was labeled as unclean (Lev. 15:19-27). "And if a woman have an issue of her blood many days out of the time of her separation, or if it run beyond the time of her separation; all the days of the issue of her uncleanness shall be as the days of her separation: *she shall be unclean*" (Lev. 15:25) (emphasis mine).

"Being unclean she was restricted in her social contacts and thus prevented from participating in worship ceremonies at the Temple. Also her synagogue attendance would be restricted if not altogether prevented."[24] It must have been lonely for her to no longer partake in the ceremonial worship with her own people.

The Bleeding Woman knew trouble could flare up if anyone discovered her secret; yet, out of desperation, she risked the exposure to see Jesus. "With the Levitical rules ordering her separation from society, she would be taking a big risk of being caught…this would result in her being exposed and removed from the crowd."[25]

The Bleeding Woman lived during the old covenant, a time when the people had to abide by the Levitical Law. It may sound unfair for her to be labeled unclean, yet the Lord designed the "clean, unclean" system to help the people understand the difference between holy and unholy (Lev. 10:10). People needed to understand their sin so they would understand their need for a Savior. When Jesus died on the cross, God ripped the veil in the temple from top to bottom (Matt. 27:51), a sign that people no longer needed a priest to intercede on their behalf. Now, in the time of the new covenant, we can have our own personal access to God.

Our access is a privilege. Did you know that Jesus' blood bought us the privilege for us to have direct access to God's presence (Heb. 10:19)? "Let us therefore come boldly unto the throne of grace, that we may obtain mercy, and find grace to help in time of need" (Heb. 4:16). Do you need some grace right now? Your boldness can take you right to God's presence on a throne of grace. What a privilege!

Our access comes from confidence in Him. Do you remember how Queen Esther felt nervous, uncertain, and starved from fasting when she approached King Ahasuerus? That's NOT how it is when we access the Lord. "Cast not away therefore your confidence" (Heb. 10:35). In other words, we are not to be timid, disheartened, or discouraged; we are to be bold. Are you confident in the Lord? Then you can trust Him. "He who trusts most strongly will enjoy the most freedom of access to God."[26]

Boldness in our Testimony

The Bleeding Woman's heart beat faster when she spotted Jesus. The closer she moved, the thicker the crowd. In her physically weak and disabled condition, she "came in the press behind" (Mark 5:27). The word *press* describes how the multitudes pressed around Jesus "so as almost to suffocate Him. The pressure was so great that it was difficult for Him to even breathe."[27]

As the Bleeding Woman neared closer to Jesus, she reached out "and touched the hem of his garment: For she said within herself, If I may but touch his garment, I shall be whole" (Matt. 9:20-21). The word *hem* doesn't mean the bottom of His garment like it would for our skirts today. Instead, it refers to the little tassels or fringes that hung on the corners of the upper part of the robe.[28]

She touched Jesus, and "immediately her issue of blood stanched [dried up]" (Luke 8:44). In amazement, she felt her blood stop flowing and knew Jesus healed her! Lickety-split she disappeared back into the crowd! But Jesus, who understood everything that happened, couldn't let her get away.

He asked, "Who touched me? When all denied, Peter and they that were with him said, Master, the multitude throng thee and press thee, and sayest thou, Who touched me? And Jesus said, Somebody hath touched me: for I perceive that virtue is gone out of me" (Luke 8:45-46).

Up to this point, the Bleeding Woman has taken risks and been bold; but now that she's healed, she clams up! Jesus knew that, due to the nature of her disease, she needed to tell everyone in the crowd His miracle (she couldn't physically prove her healing). Her testimony could help strengthen other people's faith (like Jairus who's heartbroken for his dying daughter).

A few months ago I posted on Facebook a testimony of the Lord's healing in my son's life. Hardy had an autoimmune disease in 2015; every week out of every month he would have high fevers. On Wednesday night, September 30th, another fever episode began. The day after, Hardy woke up fever free; he told me that Jesus walked around in his room that night (!) and he wasn't sick anymore. On the six month anniversary of Hardy's healing, I knew God wanted me to share Hardy's story. But I hesitated; what if his sickness came back? What if my friends thought we were wacko? I gave my excuses to the Lord, and He kept prompting me to share it. I did; I gave God all the glory for what He did in Hardy's life. God used the testimony of Hardy's healing to be a blessing to so many of my friends. Several shared with me how it helped strengthen their faith.

You have people in your own crowd that watch you, some saved and some unsaved. No matter where they are at spiritually, they need to know about the Lord's blessings in your life. You have people that love you and pray for you; they need to know when the Lord's at work in your life. Your testimony can influence someone to be saved or help strengthen another believer's faith.

Philippians 1:20 says, "But that with all boldness, as always, so now also Christ shall be magnified in my body, whether it be by life, or by death." Is your life a bold testimony of all the Lord does for you?

Boldness from Jesus' Promises

The crowd quieted to hear the Bleeding Woman's story. With "fearing and trembling" (Mark 5:33), she shared her embarrassing secret. She publicly "declared unto him before all the people for what cause she had touched him, and how she was healed immediately" (Luke 8:47).

Jesus responded, "Daughter, thy faith hath made thee whole; go in peace, and be whole of thy plague" [which literally means a whip] (Mark 5:34). She rejoiced to hear Him call her "whole," a bold promise her disease would never come back; He also called her Daughter (the only woman He ever did), a promise of a personal relationship with Him.

More commotion stirred the crowd when some messengers told Jairus his daughter died. Jesus told him, "Fear not: believe only, and she shall be made whole" (Luke 8:50). The Bleeding Woman felt relief at the timing of Jesus' announcement; it took everyone's attention off her and back on Jesus. She left, no longer a bleeding woman but now a healed woman! Did she see the priest seven days later for him to proclaim her "clean" (Lev. 15:29) and make an atonement for her since Jesus made her clean? Maybe she realized the last 12 years of her health issues were worth it since they brought her closer to the Lord.

She went to the Lord in boldness, and He gave her bold promises back. When we go to the Lord in boldness, He gives us bold promises back. Here are two:

❀ A Promise of a Personal Relationship

The day we accepted Jesus as our Savior, God became our Father. We "received the Spirit of adoption, whereby we cry, Abba, Father" (Rom. 8:15). *Abba* is another word for "Daddy." God is our Daddy and He wants us to spend time with Him. Do you need someone to talk and pour your heart out to? Your Daddy would love to hear from you!

❀ A Promise of Peace

Peace only comes from the Lord. Philippians 4:6-7 says, "Be careful for nothing; but in every thing by prayer and supplication with thanksgiving let your requests be made known unto God. And the peace of God, which passeth all understanding, shall keep your hearts and minds through Christ Jesus." Peace comes when we boldly commit our needs to the Lord. Do you feel anxious and want peace? Boldly draw closer to the Lord, and He will give you peace!

The Bleeding Woman's Roots and Fruits

Did you know someone made a stature to honor the Bleeding Woman? Church historian Eusebius wrote that he saw with his own eyes a pair of bronze statues—one of the Bleeding Woman, kneeling with arms reaching out, and the second of Jesus, arms outstretched to her. Eusebius claims that at the bottom of Jesus' statue a plant "climbs up to the hem of the brazen cloak, and is a remedy for all kinds of diseases."[29] Throughout the years, the testimony of the Bleeding Woman's boldness continues to be an encouragement to so many who struggle with health issues!

How can you grow in your season of health issues?

When I was 16 years old, I began to experience chest pain followed by hours of vomiting. The Army doctors brushed me off; they said I ate five pieces of pizza so of course I had indigestion. The next six months my attacks worsened until I discovered my gallbladder needed to be taken out. During this time, I grew in the Lord. I began to read my Bible on my own even though my family read through the Bible together every night. I talked to the Lord when I walked to school and found Him to be a good listener and comfort to me. At the time I thought it was bad timing to have health issues in my teenage years. Now I look back and believe with all my heart that my health issues were a spiritual wake-up call for me. I believe they became the best thing to happen to me as a teenager because I grew closer in my relationship to the Lord.

Our health issues can either make us bitter and drift from the Lord, or give us a boldness to draw closer to Him (Ps. 119:71). Christian boldness is wasted unless we use it to grow closer to the

Lord. The more we grow in our boldness, the more we will grow in Him.

Digging Deeper

Memorize Ephesians 3:12: *"In whom we have boldness and access with confidence by the faith of him."*

Branching Out

1. How can fear affect your faith, and faith affect your boldness?

   _____

   _____

2. According to Psalm 73:28, what happens when we draw closer to the Lord? _____

   _____

3. How can you have peace even if you are in pain? _____

   _____

   _____

4. Do you struggle with health issues? How can your boldness help you in this time? _____

   _____

I can grow in my season of health issues by _____

_____

_____

Chapter Four

Growing Stronger in Our Inner Strength

Season: Being a Wife

Zipporah and Mrs. Phinehas

Last June, Tim and I celebrated eleven years of marriage. Our marriage has been wonderful but far from perfect. "There is no such thing as a perfect marriage because it is made of imperfect people. God is the only one that is perfect and having Him in the middle of your marriage guarantees perfection in all the imperfect circumstances."[30]

A marriage consists of two people, but it really involves three—the wife, husband, and the Lord. When two saved people unite in holy matrimony, Christ by His Spirit joins them. Do you ever feel alone in your marriage? Just remember that the Lord dwells with and inside you; deep inside you and every saved person lives the "inner man." *The inner man is the real you; it's your spirit, soul, who you are deep down—the eternal part.*[31] Ephesians 3:16 says, "That he [God] would grant you, according to the riches of his glory, to be strengthened with might by his Spirit in the inner man."

Your inner man is the secret to your inner strength. Your husband's spiritual condition can influence you to be spiritually weak or strong, but what you are like on the inside will be up to you—not him. Two wives whose spiritual conditions were different than their husbands are Zipporah and Mrs. Phinehas. Zipporah was a spiritually weak woman even though her husband grew to become a great Jewish leader. Mrs. Phinehas was married to an ungodly and wicked man, yet she possessed a strong inner strength.

Inner strength comes from spiritual growth of the inner man.
Zipporah—Ex. 2:21

Zipporah's family tree dates back to Abraham and his second wife Keturah. Known as Midianites, Zipporah and her family lived in the desert land on the eastern side of the eastern gulf of the Red Sea. Her father Reuel, whose name means "friend of God," served as a priest of Midian. It appears her family believed in the one true God.[32]

Zipporah worked in the family as a shepherdess along with her six sisters. When she and her sisters went to a well to get water for their sheep, some bullying shepherds appeared, took their water, and "drove them away" (Ex. 2:17). A man named Moses witnessed the injustice and came to their rescue; he even helped them give water to their sheep. Can you imagine the excitement level of the seven girls when a hero stood up to defend them?

Zipporah and her sisters hurried to share the news of their rescue with their dad. Reuel sensed an opportunity and questioned why the girls didn't invite the stranger over for dinner. He told them to hurry up, find the hero, and bring him back home! Moses came at the invitation and stayed with Zipporah's family. She learned Moses was Jewish but grew up a prince in Egypt; he escaped from Egypt because he murdered an Egyptian man who beat up a Jew. Zipporah observed her dad's approval of Moses and soon joined him in marriage.

I remember when I was planning my wedding how much money, time, and energy I put into my outward appearance. Several times I went overboard on my clothing budget to splurge on cute skirts for the honeymoon and dresses for my upcoming role as a pastor's wife. I do believe it's important to try to look nice; I'm just acknowledging that it's easy to place more importance on our outward appearance than how we look on the inside.

It's a convicting thought—how much time, energy, and effort do you put into the spiritual growth of your inner man? A spiritually strong woman doesn't neglect the most important part of herself; she can't afford to only take care of her outward appearance. If her inner man is weak, she will be weak. If she allows the Holy Spirit to strengthen her inner man, then she will grow stronger in her inner man.

Here are some thoughts concerning our inner man:

- ❧ We are to be responsible for the condition of our inner man (also called the "hidden man of the heart" in 1 Pet. 3:4). Our soul needs a keeper, and we alone are responsible for its condition. Because the inner man is the seat of the Holy Spirit's influence, we should make its care a top priority in our life.

- ❧ We are to renew our inner man "day by day" (2 Cor. 4:16). Our outward man is dying, while our inner man continues to live and grow. We can renew our inward man with faith (v. 13), grace (v. 15), and hope (v. 18). Soul-growth and renewal won't just happen; they happen when we nourish them with God, His Word, and His strength.

Can you think of a spiritually strong woman and a spiritually weak woman? How can two women face similar circumstances, but one feels fearful and anxious while the other embraces peace and victory? What makes them different? It's their inner man—what they are really like on the inside. Ladies, let's be strong women for the Lord; let's grow in our inner strength!

Inner strength helps and sustains during the tough times.

Zipporah gave birth to a boy named Gershom and then later another boy called Eliezer. She had been married to Moses for 40 years when he came home with an announcement—God spoke to him from a burning bush and appointed him to lead the Israelite people out of bondage in Egypt.

Zipporah and her family headed west for Egypt at once. Along the way, they stopped at an inn where something mysterious happened. God almost killed Moses because their son wasn't circumcised! A sign of God's covenant with the Jewish people in Genesis 17:13-14, circumcision was a sign of God's promise to the Israelites that they would one day make it to the Promised Land. In order for the people to follow Moses to the Promised Land, they needed to know he believed in God's promises.

God could have either stricken Moses with a sickness or a death-threat with an angel.[33] Because of her husband's disability, Zipporah had to circumcise her own son! "Then Zipporah took a sharp stone, and cut off the foreskin of her son, and cast it at his feet, and said, Surely a bloody husband art thou to me. So he [God] let him [Moses] go: then she said [again!], a bloody husband thou art, because of the circumcision" (Ex. 4:25-26). "The words are clearly a reproach; and the gist of the reproach seems to be that Moses was a husband who cost her dear, causing the blood of her sons to be shed in order to keep up a national usage which she regarded as barbarous."[34]

Apparently Zipporah, the Midianite girl, had no appreciation for God's covenant with the Jewish people. The situation was an eye-opener for Moses; he firsthand saw Zipporah's true feelings about his calling and God. He sent Zipporah and the boys back home (Ex. 18:1-3).

Throughout the next year of separation in her marriage, miraculous stories of Moses circulated their way back to Zipporah's ears. She heard how God used him to deliver the two million Jewish people from Egypt, destroy Egypt and part the Red Sea, defeat the strong Amalekites, and provide food and water for the people in the desert land. Her 80-year-old husband changed from a former murderer and shepherd to a great miracle worker, emancipator, war hero, and leader of God's special nation!

When she and her family "heard of all that God had done for Moses" (Ex. 18:1), she returned back to him in the wilderness to be his wife. (Would she have returned back if the reports weren't so glowing?) Moses never recorded anything else she ever said or did after that.

Why did Zipporah crumble when the going got tough? It's because she lacked inner strength; she was weak on the inside. A spiritually strong woman doesn't quit when she faces adversity. Yes, she may feel pressed down and crushed, but with the Lord's help and strength of her inner man she will rise up and overcome.

"For our light affliction, which is but for a moment, worketh for us a far more exceeding and eternal weight of glory" (2 Cor. 4:17). As we renew our inner man, instead of quitting during the tough times, we can think about the reality and rewards in heaven. A spiritually strong woman recognizes that her "eternal weight of glory" will far outweigh any earthly sufferings.

When the tough times come (and they will), God empowers us from within. "The power of Christ within you is greater than the pressure of troubles around you."[35]   When we are strong on the inside, God helps us handle the pressures from the outside. Do you want to grow stronger in your inner strength?

Inner strength begins and grows with love.
Mrs. Phinehas—1 Samuel 2:11-17

Life in Shiloh, a city that means "peace," should have been peaceful for Mrs. Phinehas. The city had been established by Joshua to be the main worship center for the Israelites and the tabernacle permanently dwelled there (Josh. 18:1). At the tabernacle, Mrs.

Phinehas' husband Phinehas served as a priest. But Phinehas had a major problem; he, along with his brother Hophni, "knew not the LORD" (1 Sam. 2:12) and "the sin of the young men was very great before the LORD" (1 Sam. 2:17). How sad that the man who interceded for the people's sin and worship offerings didn't know the Lord! We can only imagine how Mrs. Phinehas felt.

Dear Diary, today I want to write about Phinehas. He just left for the tabernacle. He will need to get the fire hot for the offerings (Lev. 6:12) and change into his priestly clothes (Ez. 42:14). I'm glad God designed the priests' clothes to be made of fine linen so they wouldn't sweat in them (Ez. 44:18. The priestly coat looks nice with its colorful embroidered flowers (Ex. 28:40). If the clothes get stained and messy from the animal sacrifices, they will be recycled into wicks for the menorah candles and lamps."[36] I'm glad I don't have to scrub them!

Several things trouble me, though. Phinehas has been eating more meat than God allows and eats the fat before it burns (1 Sam. 2:13-16). I also discovered he's been unfaithful to me by sleeping with the women who show up to serve at the tabernacle (1 Sam. 2:22). Do any of them carry his child like I am? It's hard to feel any love towards my husband.

Ah, we finally get to talk about love! Do you remember the moment you first felt love for your husband? I do. My love moment happened when Tim and I, along with two other people, hiked the Grand Canyon. After we reached the river at the bottom, we slowly winded our way up the canyon in 122 degree weather. White streaks covered my face (from my sweat!), and I wondered if I would make it to the top. When we only had five miles to go (only!), I rested while Tim re-filled our water bottles. And that's when it hit me—I loved him! And today I am reminded that love needs more than a special memory to last—it needs to strengthen and grow.

Inner strength begins the moment you accept the Lord and His love into your life. The Holy Spirit moved into your inner man, which is the seat of His spiritual influence and where "the Holy Spirit does His renewing and saving work."[37] As Christ dwells in our heart by faith, we are to be "rooted and grounded in love...to know the love of Christ" (Eph. 3:17, 19).

Love forms the roots in our inner man and will continue as we grow in our inner man. Is it difficult for you to feel love towards your husband or someone else? Remember that God loves you and His love LIVES inside you; His love can help you love your husband or anybody else. If you're married to Mr. Almost Perfect (like me!), your love still needs to continue its growth. Yesterday's love won't guarantee today's and tomorrow's. As you grow in your love today, it will strengthen your inner man for today and tomorrow.

Inner strength gives God the glory—not us.

Mrs. Phineas' father-in-law, Eli the high priest, did nothing to restrain his sons (1 Sam. 3:13). His mild rebuke to his sons regarding their wickedness had no effect on them. God sent a prophet (1 Sam. 2:26-36) followed by a young boy named Samuel (1 Sam. 3:13-14) to prophesy to Eli the death of Phineas and Hophi. Did Mrs. Phineas ever hear about the prophecies?

To add to her stress, the Jewish people went to war with the Philistines, their neighbors to the west (1 Sam. 4:1). When the Philistines killed four thousand Israelites, the elders of Israel decided to have the ark of the covenant brought to the battlefield; they thought it could be their lucky charm. The ark, located in the tabernacle, was a large wooden chest covered in gold. It had two cherubims above it with a lid called the mercy seat (Ex. 37:1-9). Once a year, the high priest would sprinkle blood on the mercy seat to make atonement for his sins and the sins of the Israelites.

Phinehas, along with Hophni, had no qualms about moving the ark, the place of atonement for the people and symbol of God's presence, to battle. "When the ark of the covenant of the LORD came into the camp, all Israel shouted with a great shout, so that the earth rang again" (1 Sam. 4:5). This grieved the Lord and He allowed the Philistines to kill 30,000 Israelites. Hophni and Phinehas died in the battle, and the Philistines triumphed to own the Israelite's "trophy."

"And when she [Mrs. Phinehas] heard the tidings that the ark of God was taken, and that her father in law and her husband were dead, she bowed herself and travailed; for her pains came upon her" (1 Sam. 4:19). The midwives tried to comfort her and said, "Fear not; for thou hast born a son" (1 Sam. 4:20). Even after she delivered a baby boy (a crowning moment for any Jewish woman), she never even answered them. It was a "small comfort could she have of a child born in Israel, in Shiloh, when the ark is lost, and is a prisoner in the land of the Philistines."[38]

Finally she spoke and "named the child Ichabod, saying, The glory is departed from Israel: because the ark of God was taken, and because of her father in law and her husband. And she said [again!], The glory is departed from Israel: for the ark of God is taken" (1 Sam. 4:21-22). Heartache from the loss of God's glory consumed her; she then died and entered the presence and glory of the Lord. "We cannot think of the tragic death of this anonymous wife and mother…without saying that she represents many a God-fearing woman who, in spite of a shameless and godless partner, remains true to divine realities."[39]

In every relationship, God will be given glory when others see Him shine—not you—in our life. Our marriage should send a message to others that says, "Praise the Lord for all He has done for us and through us." Our relationships should never be about us and how we look. Rather, they should be about God to want to make Him look good (Ps. 90:17).

Has God's glory departed from your marriage? Though He promises to never leave your or forsake you, His glory can. Do people see God's glory in your marriage? Here's the secret of a woman with inner strength—she uses her inner strength to give God the glory (Eph. 3:21). In her marriage and in every season of life, she wants God's glory in her life so that she can give Him glory.

Zipporah's and Mrs. Phinehas's Roots and Fruits

Zipporah's husband wrote the first five books of the Bible, yet Moses chose to be mysterious regarding the rest of her life. He did mention their two sons, Gershom and Eliezer, when he recorded their genealogy in I Chronicles 23:15. Though her physical roots lived, Zipporah's spiritual roots remain weak and obscure.

Mrs. Phinehas's son Ichabod and his older brother Ahitub (1 Sam. 14:3) became priests. About 100 years later, the complete fulfillment of prophecy for the destruction of Eli and Phinehas' family did happen (2 Sam. 22:18; 1 Kings 2:27). Her family roots literally were cut off. Her spiritual fruit, however, lives today because of her grief for the departure of God's glory. Her inner strength continues to touch and bring hope to many lives of women today.

How can you grow in the season of being a wife?

If you are married, then you have an important calling in your life—to take care of and help your husband. This is no small or easy task. To successfully do this, you will need supernatural strength from the Lord. You will need to grow stronger in your inner strength. Did you know that when you grow stronger in the Lord, you will be a stronger helpmeet to your husband? A spiritually weak woman can hinder her husband while a spiritually strong woman can help him. As you strive to grow in the Lord, you will be a true helpmeet to your husband.

Digging Deeper

Memorize Ephesians 3:16: *"That he would grant you, according to the riches of his glory, to be strengthened with might by his Spirit in the inner man."*

Branching Out

1. Do you consider yourself to be a spiritually strong or a spiritually weak woman? Explain your answer._____

   _____

2. How can you renew and strengthen your inner man today?

   _____

   _____

3. What are some ways you can demonstrate your love for your husband? _____

   _____

4. According to Revelation 19:7, what will the marriage between Jesus and those who are saved bring the Lord? Does your marriage on earth do that? _____

   _____

*I can grow and bear fruit as a wife by*_____

_____

_____

Chapter Five

Grow in Remembering the Lord

Season: Dry Season

Rizpah and the Rain
2 Sam. 21:1-14

A dry season in my life began around the time my youngest daughter Selah was five months old. Her skull had shifted; the left ear went back, the left eye shrunk, the right eye and forehead puffed out, and the back right side of her head flattened. Her pediatrician diagnosed her with "plagiocephaly," a fancy name for a flat head. For 23 hours every day she had to wear a blue butterfly helmet; sweat would trickle down the back of her neck, and I ached to see that bulky, smelly thing cover up her adorable blonde hair. During that time, I maintained my quiet time with the Lord and shared my feelings in my spiritual journal. However, the Lord's presence seemed distant and voice quiet.

I could relate with the writer C.S. Lewis. After his wife died, he called out to God and sensed no reply. He asked, "What can this mean? Why is He so present a commander in our time of prosperity and so very absent a help in time of trouble?" When the questions, confusion, and loneliness come, we need to remember something—the Lord! Psalm 77:11 says, "I will remember the works of the LORD: surely I will remember thy wonders of old." In the beginning of Psalm 77, the writer felt distant from the Lord; and when He remembered the Lord, his pity party turned into a praise party!

Rizpah's dry season of life, and maybe yours, makes mine a breeze on a summer day. However, everyone's dry season comes at different times with different purposes. Rizpah's dry season brought rain to the people of Israel; let's use ours to grow closer to Him and be a blessing to others too!

Remember God's Presence

King Saul had a first wife when Rizpah married him. She became known as his concubine, a second, inferior wife (2 Sam. 3:7). A king's concubine needed to produce heirs for the throne,[40] and Rizpah gave King Saul two sons, Armoni and Mephibosheth. Outwardly, she lived a life of privilege and luxury in the royal court; inwardly, she must have dealt with many pressures in her marriage to the king.

Saul's attitude visibly changed for the worse when the Israelite women proclaimed David, the giant killer, to be their hero instead of the king. King Saul's competition with David increased; he promised his fellow tribesmen that he, not David, could give them the Gibeonites' "fields and vineyards" (1 Sam. 22:7). The Gibeonites were a group of people who 400 years earlier tricked Joshua to make a peace treaty with them (Josh. 9:19). Saul broke the deal and ordered the extinction of these people to gain favor with his people.

King Saul went to battle against the Philistines, and he died with some of his sons in the battle. The Philistines took and publicly displayed the dead bodies on a wall of Bethshan (1 Sam. 31:12). Rizpah heard some valiant men of Jabesh-Gilead (Israelites) sneaked during the night, snatched the dead bodies, burnt them, and buried them under a tree in Jabesh. Her sons no longer had a father, and she felt the lonely responsibility to take care of them.

In a dry season, we feel deserted and lonely when God feels distant. However, we need to remember we are not alone. If we have accepted Christ as our Savior, the Holy Spirit lives inside us; God promises to be with us for forever (Jn. 14:16)! Deuteronomy 31:6 says, "Be strong and of a good courage, fear not, nor be afraid of them: for the LORD thy God, he it is that doth go with thee; he will not fail thee, nor forsake thee."

Still feel alone? Here are two simple ways we can remember God's presence:

❦ Write down a time/times when you sensed God's presence. No guilt if you don't have a spiritual journal. A spiral notebook, piece of paper, or a 3x5 card to tuck in your Bible will do. The more details you can include the better. When you write down those special times, they will encourage and remind you of God's presence, like they did for the writer of Psalm 77.

❦ Fill your mind with songs, verses, and promises about God's presence. I thought I'd share a few of mine with you. My new favorite song is "You Are with Me" (sung by Christy Ingram on a cd called "God is in Command"). Three psalms I love to read about God's presence are Psalm 77, Psalm 91, and Psalm 139. One promise I love comes from Isaiah 41:10. I know filling our mind with promises of God sounds simple, but it really works. If you haven't found some verses and songs to help you, be on the lookout for those that speak to you. The more we fill our mind with thoughts and memories of God's presence, the less room there will be for thoughts of fears, doubts, and anxieties.

Remember Your Identity in the Lord

Rizpah watched the Israelite nation split into two kingdoms after Saul's death. She remained loyal to Saul's house and joined the northern kingdom (Israel), with Ishbosheth, one of Saul's sons, as king. David, the hero against the Philistines, became king of the southern kingdom (Judah).

The two kingdoms made war against each other; David's kingdom grew stronger and Saul's kingdom "waxed weaker and weaker" (2 Sam. 3:1). However, Abner, a former general of Saul's army "made himself strong for the house of Saul" (2 Sam. 3:6). Rizpah looked to Abner for security, and their relationship soon had people talking.

It must have been embarrassing for her when her new king Ishbosheth confronted Abner and accused him about their relationship (2 Sam. 3:7). Back then, to be "with a king's concubine was a treasonous act, for it was in essence making a claim to the throne."[41] Abner never denied the accusation; instead, he called Ishbosheth a fool and switched his loyalty to King David. His influence caused the people of the northern kingdom to unite with David.

Rizpah faced more sadness and heartache when the general of David's army murdered Abner. Even King David mourned the loss of Abner. The people saw David's devotion for Abner (2 Sam. 3:37), and they unified and accepted David as king. Rizpah no longer had any family ties with the royal family. She disappeared from the royal scene, no longer identified with the royal family.

As Christians, it's assuring to know that we will always have our identity in the Lord. It's not something we can lose or even create. It's something we receive, not achieve. It has nothing to do with us and everything to do with the Lord. The question is not, "Who am I?" but rather, "Whose am I?" Too often we think our identity comes from our personal accomplishments, our family background, or personal relationships. Our achievements may explain us but they don't define us. It's a relief to me to know that my identity has nothing to do with what I have done. Instead, my identity comes from the Lord and what He has done.

Unlike the world, we don't need to go through an identity crisis, "a period of uncertainty and confusion in which a person's sense of identity becomes insecure."[42] Here are some ways we can feel secure in our identity with the Lord:

- 🌸 He loves us (Jn. 17:23)
- 🌸 He forgives us (Eph. 1:7)
- 🌸 He redeems us (Rev. 5:9)
- 🌸 He adopts us to be His children (Jn. 1:12)
- 🌸 He empowers us through the Holy Spirit (Jn. 1:12)
- 🌸 He grants us citizenship to heaven (Col. 1:13)

Aren't we so blessed to have our identity in the Lord? In a dry season, it's important we remember to feel assured of our security in the Lord and our identity through Him.

Remember to Go to the Lord

Three years of a famine struck the land of Israel. Rizpah felt the pressure to provide meals for her family during the serious food and water shortage. People in Israel began to wonder why God withheld the rain, a sign of His blessing. Surely it never occurred to Rizpah that God sent the famine because of her family. She would discover the solution to end the famine would be more painful than the famine itself.

King David realized God had a reason for the famine, and he "inquired of the LORD. And the LORD answered, It is for Saul, and for his bloody house, because he slew the Gibeonites" (2 Sam. 21:1). Immediately King David arranged a meeting with the Gibeonites and said, "What shall I do for you? and wherewith shall I make the atonement, that ye may bless the inheritance of the LORD?" (2 Sam. 21:3).

The Gibeonites said they wanted no money for compensation. "And they answered the king, The man that consumed us, and that devised against us that we should be destroyed from remaining in any of the coasts of Israel, Let seven men of his sons be delivered unto us, and we will hang them up unto the LORD in Gibeah of Saul, whom the LORD did choose" (2 Sam. 21:5-6). David agreed to their terms; he ordered the death of Rizpah's sons Mephibosheth and Armoni, along with five other grandsons of King Saul.

In April, the beginning of barley harvest time, Rizpah watched the Gibeonites take her sons taken away. Her sons could have been innocent, or maybe they did have guilty dealings with the Gibeonites (the Lord referred to Saul's house as "bloody"). Either way, did Rizpah understand a pardon for sin required the shedding of blood? Everything she loved and lived for no longer belonged to her. In anguish and pain, she went to the hill and watched the Gibeonites hang her sons.

Wow, as a mother I can't imagine the pain she felt. However, God understood her pain. He allowed His innocent son Jesus to be crucified on a cross to pay for our sins. Your friends and family may not understand your struggles, but the Lord understands. In your dry season, remember the Lord and go to Him.

- *Cry to the Lord*. Psalm 77:1 says, "I cried unto God with my voice…and he gave ear unto me." The writer of Psalm 77 "cried," "sought," and "complained" (vv. 1-3). The more the Lord seemed quiet, the more noise the writer made! Have you ever had a good cry and felt better afterwards? I know I have. Cry to the Lord—you will start to feel better!

- *Confess any sin*. Psalm 77:6 says, "I call to remembrance my song in the night: I commune with mine own heart: and my spirit made diligent search." A dry season is a good time to search our heart and confess any lingering sin in our life (Ps. 139:23-24). Sin strains our relationship with the Lord and can be a cause (though not every time) of a dry season.

- *Cling to special memories with the Lord*. Psalm 77:11 says, "I will remember the works of the LORD: surely I will remember thy wonders of old." This verse has been such a blessing and a help to me. A couple months ago, I struggled with some health issues in our family. Then I remembered how the Lord delivered my son from some serious health problems last year. I believed that since the Lord did a miracle last year, He could do another one again if He wanted! When we remember the past wonders of the Lord, we will remember He can do amazing wonders for today!

Remember God Sends the Rain

Shock and anger flowed through Rizpah's body when she discovered the Gibeonites planned to leave her son's dead bodies on the pole. The Israelites always took down the hung bodies by nighttime in accordance to the law (Deut. 21:23). The disgrace of her sons' hangings (Gal. 3:13) felt even more disgraceful with the exposure of the dead bodies. She determined they would have a proper burial and personally committed to watch and protect the dead bodies.

That hill became her new home. To show her mourning, she took sackcloth, a sack or bag made up of rough, goat's hair, "and spread it for her upon the rock" (2 Sam. 21:10) to provide shelter. (The phrase *spread it for her upon the rock* implies she pitched it like she would a tent.[43]) Despite the gruesome sights and smells of the decomposing bodies, she remained steadfast on her rock and hill.

Her face was sunburned, hair tangled and wild, lips chapped, nails cracked, stomach starved, heart crushed, mental condition shot, and body physically exhausted from her 24 hour vigil. She literally looked like an animal; long gone were her royal pampered days.

Though the extreme summer heat would reach around 100 degrees with no cooling rain (2 Sam. 21:10), nothing moved Rizpah from her dry rock and hill. Every day her eyes witnessed the bodies' gradual decomposition. In the daytime, she yelled with her hoarse voice to chase predator animals away. By nighttime she probably lit

56

a torch to chase away any wild predators. (Remember this happened during a third year of famine and the animals were also starving.)

In October, about six months later, Rizpah watched King David appear on her hill; he had heard about her vigil. He arrived to collect the bones and bury them, along with Saul and his best friend Jonathan's (dug up from under a tree), in the grave of Saul's father (2 Sam. 21:14). Perhaps he thanked her for bringing to his memory a long-forgotten duty—an honorable burial of his best friend.

Rizpah felt excited to know her grueling vigil prompted the king to properly bury her sons! "And after that God was intreated for the land" (2 Sam. 21:14). The Lord sent rain to "put an end to the famine, and be regarded as a proof that the wrath of Heaven was appeased."[44] Rizpah and the people rejoiced to see God's rain end the dry season!

Isn't it a comfort to remember God sends the rain? You may ask, "When will He send my rain? When will my dry season end?" My answer is, "I don't know." In Leviticus 26:3-4, God says that as we follow Him and do what's right, He will give us "rain in due season." The phrase *due season* means God's time, not ours. We need to remember that God's timing is never late; it's always on time.

As I reflect back to my dry season with Selah and the helmet, I can't pinpoint an exact "Aha! It's raining!" moment. I heard a sermon that spoke to my heart before her first birthday; I read a book that blessed me. My dry season came to a close—even before I knew the outcome of her helmet. While the Lord seemed distant before, His presence and comfort felt so close to me then. It was raining!

Dry seasons don't always have to end after our struggles; they can finish even before then! (And here's the rest of the story—her helmet came off when she was one year old, and around 18 months her head began to look better. By the time she was two, her head measurements lined up with perfection! Thank you Lord!)

In Isaiah 44:3, the Lord said, "For I will pour water upon him that is thirsty, and floods upon the dry ground." I like how God says, "I will." He will pour water, a symbol of His Spirit and grace (Jn. 7:38), to those thirsty and spiritually dry. What a great promise to claim during a dry season!

During a time of great drought, the Scottish preacher Dr. Guthrie prayed for rain in the morning service. As he went to church in the afternoon, his daughter, Mary, said, "Here is the umbrella, Papa." "What do we need it for?" he asked. "You prayed for rain this morning, and don't you expect God will send it?" They carried the umbrella, and when they came home they were glad to take shelter under it from the drenching storm.[45]

Are you in a dry season? Grab your umbrella and pray for rain!

Rizpah's Roots and Fruits

Rizpah's faithful vigil on the dead bodies preserved the memory of her family. She didn't have an honorable family, but her actions brought honor to her family. What an inspiring example of how a woman's determined spirit can influence the heart of a king! Though her spiritual life remains a mystery, Rizpah's "noble example had borne fruit"[46] and brought blessings to the people of Israel.

How can you grow in a dry season?

Remember, if you have the Lord in your life His Spirit lives inside you; this means you have access to an unlimited water supply for your growth. When you start to feel spiritually dry, tap into your "underground water supply" for your growth. Did you know that in the Amazon rainforest some tree growth only happens during a dry season? While they soak up the rays of the sun, they extend their deep roots into a nearby water supply.[47] The Lord can make a "dry tree to flourish" (Ez. 17:24), and He can help you grow too. Let's grow in the dry times, so when the rains come we can grow some more!

Digging Deeper

Memorize Psalm 77:10-11: *"And I said, This is my infirmity: but I will remember the years of the right hand of the most High. I will remember the works of the LORD: surely I will remember thy wonders of old."*

Branching Out

1. What are some special memories and wonders the Lord did for you that you need to remember in a dry season? _____

   _____

2. In Second Samuel 21:1, what's something David did during his dry season that we should do in ours? _____

   _____

   _____

3. Have you ever gone through an "identity crisis"? How does the Lord help you feel secure in your identity through Him? _____

   _____

   _____

4. From Hosea 10:12, how can we experience God's rain? _____

   _____

   _____

I can grow and bear fruit in my dry season by_____

_____

_____

Chapter Six

Growing to Want God's Best for Your Children

Season: Motherhood

Salome
Matthew 20:20-24

I never understood a mother's love until July 21, 2006. That's the day I gave birth to my daughter Tirzah (pronounced "tears-uh"). Feelings of deep joy took a permanent place in my heart. I had to be on bed rest for five weeks with Tirzah, and we spent plenty of bonding time. The first time we left home happened to be to our church's mid-week service. I remember the first time I buckled her up in the infant car seat. In a split second, my feelings of excitement turned to concern. What if we got in a car accident, or she choked on baby spit-up? She looked so small, so vulnerable for all that lied ahead. I wanted to shield her, to never let anything bad happen to her. In that one moment, my bright view of motherhood dimmed.

God has blessed me and Tim with four adorable children—Tirzah (10), Hardy (8), Acarith (6, pronounced "uh-care-ith"), and Selah (4). I love my children and want the best things to happen to them. Still, the more I try to grow in motherhood, the more I realize that my best for them may be different than God's best. God said, "For my thoughts are not your thoughts, neither are your ways my ways, saith the LORD" (Is. 55:8).

Like most mothers, Salome wanted the best for her sons James and John. When she asked Jesus to grant her sons the best thing she could imagine, she learned God's best differed from her best. "But there is also great encouragement connected with the story of Salome. God knows what is really best for a child and He wants to provide it, even when the mother asks for the wrong thing."[48]

Do you want God's best for your children?
Give them to the Lord.

Salome and her husband Zebedee rejoiced when she gave birth to their firstborn son James. Another son named John joined the family, and Salome felt double blessed. While she stayed at home with the boys, Zebedee managed a fishing business on the Sea of Galilee. (Josephus the historian wrote that during this time one fishing fleet numbered 240 fishing boats.[49]) Zebedee's fishing business grew to hire servants (Mark 1:20), and Salome and Zebedee probably planned for their boys to one day take over the family business.

The family of Zebedee lived in Capernaum, a coastal community along the western shore of the Sea of Galilee. Life for Salome's family might have been idyllic, except for one thing—they, along with thousands of other Jewish families, lived under the harsh rule of the Roman government. Salome longed for the day the Messiah, a man that prophets hundreds of years earlier foretold, would defeat the Romans and establish a peaceful, earthly kingdom at Jerusalem. She also knew Isaiah the prophet wrote about a spiritual revival that would happen in Galilee (Is. 9:1-2).

Salome and her family participated in the Jewish ceremonies at their temple in Jerusalem to worship the Lord. They even had connections with the high priest, a respected authority in the land (Jn. 18:15-16). When James and John began to follow a man named John the Baptist who preached fiery messages of repentance, Salome and Zebedee gave their approval. Later, the brothers began to follow Jesus when John the Baptist pointed to Him and said, "Behold the Lamb of God!" (Jn. 1:36).

Salome personally had a love and dedication for the Lord, and she encouraged her sons to be passionate about spiritual matters as well. It's highly possible she and Zebedee gave their children to the

Lord since it was a common practice among other Jewish moms and dads (see 1 Sam. 1:27; Luke 1:57-66; Luke 2:22; Gen. 22).

When each of our children was born, Tim and I gave them to the Lord. I'll confess, however, there have been times in my heart when I took them back from the Lord and then had to give them back to Him. I mean, it was hard to accept I couldn't give them my best in life—I had to surrender them to God's best. Do you know what I mean? This is when we need to remember the Lord's best, His plan and will, is truly what's best.

Here's what it means to give your children to the Lord. (I wish it were as easy to do as it sounds!)

🌾 You confirm your love and dedication to God (Matt. 10:37-38)
🌾 You acknowledge they don't belong to you but to God (Ps. 127:3-5)
🌾 You commit to raising them for the Lord (Eph. 6:4)
🌾 You believe in God's promises in your life (Heb. 11:17)

The longer I am a mother, the more I realize motherhood isn't about me—it's about the Lord and His work through my family. Motherhood is something the Lord gives to us so we can give back to Him. Have you ever given your children to the Lord?

Do you want God's best for your children?
Teach them how to listen, obey, and follow God's call.

Salome's sons followed Jesus, in a casual sense, while they remained in the family fishing business. It saddened the family to hear King Herod threw John the Baptist into prison. However, something good did come from John the Baptist's imprisonment— Jesus moved the base of His ministry to Galilee (Matt. 4:13). Isaiah's prophecy became fulfilled for the people of Galilee.

"And Jesus went about all Galilee, teaching in their synagogues, and preaching the gospel of the kingdom, and healing all manner of sickness and all manner of disease among the people…And there followed him great multitudes of people from Galilee" (Matt. 4:23, 25a). Salome, too, became a follower of Jesus.

While Jesus walked on the shore of the beautiful Sea of Galilee, He "saw other two brethren, James the son of Zebedee, and John his brother, in a ship with Zebedee their father, mending their nets; and he called them. And they immediately left the ship and their father, and followed him" (Matt. 4:21-22). At this point, James and John already knew and followed Jesus. Yet, they understood He was calling them again to intensify their discipleship.

Eventually, Jesus called her sons five times for different purposes. (As we compare the four gospels, He called them in John 1:29, Matthew 4:18, Luke 5:11, Mark 3:14, and Matthew 10:1.) Salome and Zebedee knew the day when both of their sons were serious—they quit the family fishing business to be fishers of men with Jesus (Luke 5:9-10).

Do you see how each calling progressed and raised their commitment to a higher level? God's call works the same with us. After we accept His call of salvation, He calls us to a level of obedience (baptism); then He calls us to different levels of commitment (like a specific ministry, place, or people). We need to remember God's calling isn't just for us—He also has a calling for our children. As mothers, it's important that we teach them how to listen, obey, and follow God's call. Here are two ways we can do this:

- By our example. As our children watch us respond to the Lord's calling in our life, they will have a better understanding when He calls them. Yes, a child can respond to God's calling without any spiritual examples from their home, but the more they watch and learn from our example, the more they will be confident and encouraged. Did you know that when Jesus calls us, He actually left us a godly example to "follow his steps"? (1 Pet. 2:21). Likewise, we need to set the godly example for our children to follow in His steps.

🌿 By our training. As we train our children to listen and obey us, they will learn to listen and obey the Lord. "Withhold not correction from the child...Thou shalt beat him with the rod, and shalt deliver his soul from hell" (Prov. 23:13-14). We can't expect our child to say "yes" to God if he or she says "no" to us. I know training our children can be hard, tiresome, and time consuming, but we must understand then our training will prepare our children to know how to respond to God's call.

Do you want God's best for your children?
Encourage them to have ambition for the Lord.

For the next three years Salome continued to follow and support Jesus. "Because of her family's affluence, Salome would have been able to join her sons for extended periods of time...helping meet logistical, practical, and financial needs."[50] She felt proud to know that Jesus chose both James and John to be a part of His inner circle of close companions. How she longed for the day Jesus would defeat the cruel Romans and establish His earthly kingdom!

Salome saw marks of spiritual growth in both of her sons from Jesus and His influence. Though they had much to learn, they did have a passion for the Lord. Her older son James had a fiery personality[51] and a way of stirring things up (Luke 9:51-56). Jesus taught James about loving kindness and steered James' passion in the right spiritual direction. John also had a similar temperament. "He was passionate, zealous, and personally ambitious—just like his brother James. They were cut from the same bolt of cloth. But John aged well."[52] John learned much about love from the Lord.

The Passover Feast drew near, and Salome and her sons walked with Jesus to Judea to join the celebration. Along the way, Jesus shared sobering news with His disciples. "Behold, we go up to Jerusalem; and the Son of man shall be betrayed unto the chief priests and unto the scribes, and they shall condemn him to death, And shall deliver him to the Gentiles to mock, and to scourge, and to crucify him: and the third day he shall rise again" (Matt. 20:18-19).

At that moment, Salome approached Him "with her sons, worshipping him, and desiring a certain thing of him" (Matt. 20:20). Jesus asked her what she needed, and she said, "Grant that these my two sons may sit, the one on thy right hand, and the other on the left, in thy kingdom" (Matt. 20:21).

Wow! Salome had big plans for her sons, didn't she? "Salome was ambitious for her sons, and ambition is commendable when it is in full agreement with the mind and purpose of God."[53] Unfortunately, her ambition centered on self-promotion and recognition for her sons. It wasn't God's ambition, nor was it God's best for her sons.

Ambition can be either good or bad. It all depends on who we want to please the most with our ambition—ourselves or God. The apostle Paul had godly ambition when he said, "Wherefore we labour, that, whether present or absent, we may be accepted of him" (2 Cor. 5:9). The word *labour* in this verse is another word for ambition. Our ambition for God pleases Him when it promotes Him and gives Him glory.

As mothers, we like to make big plans for our kids, don't we? Or maybe our kids are already making their own big plans in life. Mine like to say, "When I grow up, I want to be a _____." My daughter Acarith wants to own her own bakery; Selah wants to be a mommy to fifty babies. And me? Well, I don't know what God wants them to do. I just encourage each of them to do what God wants them to do, and to do it for Him and His glory.

Ambitions and big dreams are great to have when used for the Lord. Here's a good question to ask about ambitions—"Does my or my child's ambition seek to promote the Lord or self?" If it's for self-promotion, don't encourage it. If it's for the Lord, it still might not be God's best, but it's a good place to start.

Do you want God's best for your children?
Trust how and where the Lord leads them.

Jesus replied to Salome's request, "Ye know not what ye ask. Are ye able to drink of the cup that I shall drink of, and to be baptized with the baptism that I am baptized with? They say unto him, We are able" (Matt. 20:22). Jesus didn't deny Salome's requests. Instead, He corrected it.[54]

He said, "Ye shall drink indeed of my cup, and be baptized with the baptism that I am baptized with: but to sit on my right hand, and on my left, is not mine to give, but it shall be given to them for whom it is prepared of my Father" (Matt. 20:23). The other ten disciples heard this and felt angry! What gave the sons of Zebedee any right to special privileges? They, too, had forsaken all to follow the Lord's call.

A few days later, Salome grieved when her own people gave Jesus to the Romans to crucify Him on the cross (Mark 15:40). Her son John kept his distance, and James hid from the scene. "Salome's dreams of the kingship of Christ with her sons sharing His rule were rudely shattered as she saw her much-loved Messiah dying as a felon on a wooden gibbet."[55] When Jesus died on the cross, so did all her hopes and plans for the future.

On sunrise Sunday, the third day of His death, she and other women sneaked their way to the tomb. They intended to anoint His dead body with sweet spices until an angel told them Jesus had risen from the dead (Mark 16:1-6)! Salome and her friends were in total shock over the miracle! For the next 40 days, Jesus lived on earth until He ascended up to heaven. She and her family continued to follow Jesus with more of a passion than ever before. They put aside their own selfish ambitions to preach the good news of Jesus' death, resurrection, and love.

Her firstborn son James drank from his cup of suffering when he became the first apostle martyr of the early church. History records that the man who led James to the judgment seat felt convicted by James' bold testimony and confessed that he, too, was a Christian. The executioner beheaded him alongside James.[56] John drank his cup of suffering in a different way; he outlived his fellow disciples, who died martyred deaths, and lived a lonely life of his later years in exile on an island. In some ways, that may have been the most painful suffering of all.

We don't know how much suffering Salome faced or eye witnessed in her son's lives. We do know that Salome had to accept and trust God's leading for her sons. She had instilled in her boys' life a passion for the Lord, and the time had come for her to entrust them with Him.

"Lo, children are an heritage of the LORD: and the fruit of the womb is his reward. As arrows are in the hand of a mighty man; so are children of the youth. Happy is the man that hath his quiver full of them" (Ps. 127:3-5a). The quiver is the case which held the arrows until they were eventually pulled out, aimed, and then released.

Our children are like arrows. They are made and being sharpened with a purpose to release and use. We can't keep them by our side for the rest of our life; that would be useless. Their will come a time when we need to aim and release them to God's best, His plan. Like arrows that are shot, we can aim and release our children to where we think is best and trust where God leads them.

We don't know where God may lead our children, our arrows. "God always gives His best to those who leave the choice to Him."[57] He may lead them to health struggles, family problems, or spiritual suffering. Maybe He will lead them to be missionaries to a remote corner of the world. Yes, there's a cost. But our motherhood and discipleship for the Lord should reach people for the Lord with what He has given us.

"So, with the strong arms of prayer, draw the bowstring back and let the arrows fly—all of them, straight at the enemy's hosts."[58] As our children soar, we can trust God will lead them to His best for them.

Salome's Roots and Fruits

In a spiritual sense, the Zebedee family fishing business is still in business today. Her sons still cast nets into the sea of the world through their testimony in the Gospels and epistles; they still bring people to the Lord. John wrote, aside from Luke and Paul, "more of the New Testament than any other human author."[59] Salome's boys reveal the powerful testimony a mother has who wants God's best for her children—not her own. Her life shows how a mother's roots and fruits can reach out to many others when she gives her children to the Lord.

How can you grow in the season of motherhood?

It's not easy being a mother. (Do I hear an amen?) And it's certainly no easy thing to surrender our personal rights of our children over to the Lord. And yet, when we do, we grow. We grow in our trust in the Lord and from our submission to Him. Jim Elliot said, "He is no fool who gives what he cannot keep to gain what he cannot lose." To paraphrase that in mommy language, "You are a wise mother if you give your child back to the Lord; and what you thought you would lose, you will actually gain."

Digging Deeper

Memorize Isaiah 40:11: *"He shall feed his flock like a shepherd: he shall gather the lambs with his arm, and carry them in his bosom, and shall gently lead those that are with young."*

Branching Out

1. What are some ways you can encourage your child to have godly ambitions? _____

   _____

2. In First Samuel 1:27-28, what did Hannah learn about the Lord? What did she do in return? _____

   _____

   _____

3. Do your thoughts and actions show that you trust your child in the Lord's care? _____

   _____

4. Have you ever verbally given your children to the Lord? If not, I would encourage you to do so today. Write down the day you gave your children to the Lord in a journal or the back of the Bible as a reminder of your commitment. _____

   _____

I can grow and bear fruit as a mother by_____

_____

_____

Chapter Seven

Growing to Sow Seeds and Reap Souls

Seasons of Sowing and Reaping

The Samaritan Woman
John 4

A young farmer stands in his field and observes a peculiar cloud formation. The clouds form the letters G, P, and C, and he thinks them a call from God to *Go preach Christ!* The farmer rushes to the deacons of his church and insists that he has been called to preach. Respectful of his zeal, they invite him to fill the pulpit. That Sunday the long and boring sermon finally ends, and the leaders sit in stunned silence. Finally, a wise deacon mutters to the would-be preacher, "Seems to me the clouds were saying 'Go plant corn.'"

Sometimes we think like the farmer. We wonder what the Lord wants us to do for Him; other times, we don't understand the results we see from our hard work. In the season of sowing, we plant gospel seeds about the Lord to those who need to accept Him as their Savior and leave the results up to the Lord. In the season of reaping, we lead people to the Lord ready to receive Him as their Savior. You may be a sower, a reaper, or both. Both seasons need to work together to have a successful harvest.

Jesus, the great Sower, spread a gospel seed to the Samaritan Woman. She believed in Christ and sowed gospel seeds to everyone in her hometown. Both Jesus and His disciples reaped the lost souls for Him. Many people, and then "many more" (Jn. 4:41), in the Samaritan Woman's village came to know the Lord through the hard work of both the sowers and reapers!

Sowers sow seeds everywhere—
and leave the results up to God.

The Samaritan Woman knew the Jewish people hated her and her people. About 700 years earlier, the Assyrians invaded northern Israel and established colonies; the Babylonians did the same to southern Israel (2 Kings 17:1-6) and also kidnapped the Jews to Babylon. The intermarriages between the Jews, Assyrians, and Babylonians formed a new group of people called Samaritans. Seventy years later, the kidnapped Jews in Babylon returned to their homeland (Ezra 1:1-3), furious to discover the "half-breed" Samaritans who lived in Samaria. The Jews established homes north of Samaria (an area called Galilee) and to the south (an area called Judea). If the Jews needed to travel from Galilee to Judea (or vice versa), they never took the short cut through Samaria. They would travel all around Samaria to escape interaction with the people.

It must have been a challenge for the Samaritan Woman to live sandwiched between people who hated her. She became used to the feuds and maintained a personal distance from the Jews. Did she ever hear stories in Samaria about Jesus, a man who performed miracles primarily for the Jews in Galilee and Judea?

Unfortunately, the Jews in Judea rejected Jesus and He decided to head north to be with the people of Galilee. He could have traveled east towards the Jordan River and then up to Galilee, like the other Jews did. But He didn't. He decided "he must needs go through Samaria" (Jn. 4:4). His disciples joined him for the 20 mile journey, and around noontime they arrived in Sychar, the Samaritan Woman's hometown. Jesus rested at Jacob's Well, a 100 ft. deep well, while the hungry disciples went to buy lunch.

The Samaritan Woman carried her water pot as she walked the half-mile from outside her city to Jacob's Well. Her village had plenty springs of water, but she may not have been allowed to use them because of her bad reputation.[60] When she arrived at the well with her water pot, she felt shocked to see a Jewish man sitting there!

He said, "Give me to drink" (Jn. 4:7). With no hesitation, she said, "How is it that thou, being a Jew, askest drink of me, which am a woman of Samaria? for the Jews have no dealings with the Samaritans" (v. 9). Since the word *dealings* literally means "to use vessels together," she's amazed Jesus wants to drink from her own water pot! She's literally an outcast from the outcasts—a sad place to be. She has no idea that He, God of the universe, planned this meeting to sow seeds in her life!

Jesus wants us to learn by His example that sowers need to sow seeds everywhere. In Luke 8:5-8, Jesus told a parable about a sower who sowed seed. Some seed fell by the way side, some fell on rocks and thorns, and some on good ground. Only the seed on the good ground "sprang up, and bare fruit" (Luke 8:8). A couple things we can learn from this parable about sowing are:

- ❧ The seed represents "the word of God" (Luke 8:11).
- ❧ The way side, rocks, and thorns represent those that rejected the seed's power (Luke 8:12-14).
- ❧ The good ground represents the "honest and good heart" that keeps the seed and will bring forth fruit (Luke 8:15).

By all outward appearances, the Samaritan Woman was an unlikely candidate to receive seed, but Jesus knew her heart. Admittedly, Jesus has an advantage over us in that He knows everything about everyone. And yet, since we don't know what goes on inside people's hearts, we should try to reach everyone with our gospel seeds.

A sower spreads gospel seed everywhere—even to the outcasts. "He that observeth the wind shall not sow...In the morning sow thy seed, and in the evening withhold not thine hand: for thou knowest not whether shall prosper, either this or that, or whether they both shall be alike good" (Eccl. 11:4a, 6). If we only sow seeds under ideal conditions, we'll probably never sow them. Sowers shouldn't think, "I'm not going to plant this seed because it won't help that person." Sowers need to think, "I'm going to plant this seed because I know God can use it to help that person." Sowers sow seeds and leave the results up to God!

Sowers sow gospel seeds.

The Samaritan Woman knew this Man broke all social barriers when He talked to her. It was unheard of for Jews to talk to Samaritans, men to women in public, and religious leaders to prostitutes. Jesus continued, "If thou knewest the gift of God, and who it is that saith to thee, Give me to drink; thou wouldest have asked of him, and he would have given thee living water" (Jn. 4:10).

She feels confused by His reply; He told her she needs to get water from Him! She reminds Him that He's the one without a water pot, and He couldn't get the well water without it. Jesus said, "Whosoever drinketh of this water shall thirst again: But whosoever drinketh of the water that I shall give him shall never thirst; but the water that I shall give him shall be in him a well of water springing up into everlasting life" (vv. 13-14).

She had an "Aha!" moment and understood the water had a spiritual meaning. "Sir, give me this water, that I thirst not, neither come hither to draw" (v. 15). She must have thought it would be wonderful to not have to walk so far to get water and have a daily reminder of her sinful life.

Instead of Jesus granting her eternal life, He brought up her sinful past. He told her, "Go, call thy husband, and come hither" (v. 16). Maybe she wanted Him to think she was a widow or a single woman when she gave a short reply, "I have no husband" (v. 17). Jesus kindly rebuked her and said, "Thou hast well said, I have no husband: For thou hast had five husbands; and he whom thou now hast is not thy husband: in that saidst thou truly" (vv.17-18).

Gulp! I guess it's kind of nice to not know everyone's story when we talk to them! Jesus didn't pretend to be oblivious about the Samaritan Woman's story—He knew all about her. He had to bring up her sinful lifestyle so she could acknowledge her need for a Savior—a topic all sowers need to bring up when they sow gospel seeds in someone else' life.

Last year, a homely looking woman approached me and my girls inside Wal-Mart. Her breath reeked of alcohol (which says a lot since I don't have a good smeller) and I wanted to leave. She talked to me, and I tried to make small talk with her back. The Holy Spirit whispered to me, "Give her a tract." I didn't want to; I didn't want her to visit our church (terrible of me, I know). Again the Lord talked to me and reminded me she needs Him. I reached into my purse, gave her a tract, and invited her to church. Guess what? She all of a sudden remembered the item she was looking for and hurried away! I feel ashamed that I didn't want to sow a seed, but I'm so glad I listened and obeyed the Lord. I don't know if she read the tract, but I do know I can leave the results of the harvest up to the Lord.

We need to sow gospel seeds in people's hearts. Gospel means "good news;" don't you love to hear good news? Well, let's love to spread some good news!

- The gospel news begins with bad news—everyone is born a sinner (Rom. 3:23) and their sin earns them death (Rom. 6:23).
- Then comes good news—Jesus loves them so much He died on the cross and rose again to give them eternal life.
- And more good news—whoever calls on Jesus to be their Savior will be saved (Rom. 10:13). Amen! That's the truth people need to hear.

Anyone can be a sower of gospel seeds and in a season of sowing. Let's make sure we follow the Lord's promptings and sow those seeds. Gospel seeds get planted when we tell others the good news of Jesus Christ!

Reapers finish the job of the sower.

The Samaritan Woman both marveled and squirmed that the stranger knew about her. She quickly switched the subject back to Him. "Sir, I perceive that thou art a prophet. Our fathers worshipped in this mountain; and ye say, that in Jerusalem is the place where men ought to worship" (Jn. 4:19-20). She never went to Jerusalem to worship in the Jewish temple. If she did worship, she went to Mount Gerizim where Sanballat, a former enemy of Nehemiah and the Jews, had built a temple for the Samaritans "and instituted a priesthood, as rivals to those of the Jews at Jerusalem."[61]

Jesus redirected her thoughts from a place of worship to a Person of worship. "Woman, believe me, the hour cometh, when ye shall neither in this mountain, nor yet at Jerusalem, worship the Father. Ye worship ye know not what: we know what we worship: for salvation is of the Jews [Jesus was a Jew and salvation would come by Him.]" (vv. 21-22). He told her God the Father wanted to be worshipped in spirit and truth.

She said, "I know that Messias cometh, which is called Christ: when he is come, he will tell us all things. Jesus saith unto her, I that speak unto thee am he" (vv. 25-26). Boy, did she get excited; the man she talked with was the Messiah! She left her water pot and ran the half mile back to her city. She told the men (she knew about them and they knew about her), "Come, see a man, which told me all things that ever I did [She acknowledges her sin which indicates her salvation.[62]]: is not this the Christ?" (v. 29). The men, curious about the change in her, left the city to meet Jesus at the well.

Meanwhile, the disciples returned with lunch for Jesus. They marveled that He talked with the Samaritan Woman (nobody dared ask why!). Jesus refused to eat the lunch they brought and said, "I have meat to eat that ye know not of" (v. 32). When the disciples wondered who brought Him food, Jesus repeated what He said to them and added "…and to *finish* his work" (v. 34) (emphasis mine).

In a farming community, the reapers gather up and finish everything the sowers did from planting season. The reapers have been eyeballing the crops and know they are ready to be gathered up. The same principle for sowers applies spiritually. A spiritual reaper comes along, sees someone ripe with the gospel seed, and leads them to the Lord. The reapers finish the job the sowers started. There's a beautiful picture of teamwork here by sowers and reapers. Sowers start, reapers finish.

The success of the harvest depends on them both. It's impossible for a reaper to reap something not sown, and it's impossible for a sower to reap every seed sown. I don't know about you, but this thought brings me so much comfort. God's kingdom depends on me, but it isn't all on me. I work with you, and you work with me. Together we can accomplish much for the Lord of the harvest.

Have you taught kids at church, mingled with women at Bible studies, knocked on doors to share the gospel, invited people to church, handed out gospel tracts, sung in church, prayed for lost souls, or visited people in nursing homes? Many of the people you have been around you may never have the opportunity to be with again. But guess what, my fellow sower and reaper? I have some comforting news. You may one day reap what you have sown. Or, you may reap what I have sown. And one day, I may reap what you have sown. Reapers, let's finish the job of the sowers!

Reapers work in God's timing.

Jesus knew that soon the Samaritans would join Him at the well; there would be souls ready to reap for the harvest. He said, "And herein is that saying true, One soweth, and another reapeth. I sent you to reap that whereon ye bestowed no labour: other men laboured, and ye are entered into their labours [the Samaritan Woman]" (Jn. 4: 37-38).

Did the Samaritan Woman go back to the well with the other Samaritans to be with Jesus, or did she stay in town to spread more gospel news? "And **many** of the Samaritans of that city believed on him for the saying of the woman, which testified, He told me all that ever I did" (v. 39) (emphasis mine).

The Samaritans invited Jesus to stay with them. He accepted their invitation and stayed with them for two more days. "And **many more** believed because of his own word" (v. 41) (emphasis mine). People told the Samaritan Woman, "Now we believe, not because of thy saying: for we have heard him ourselves, and know that this is indeed the Christ, the Saviour of the world" (v. 42). The Samaritan Woman's changed life and love for the Lord compelled her to be a sower and a reaper for Him!

Talk about a reaper's dream—people flocking to Jesus, ready to listen and receive Him! Reapers work hard for the Lord and know when it's time to reap. Three ways to reap in God's timing are—

❀ Look on the fields. Jesus told His disciples, his fellow reapers, "Lift up your eyes, and look on the fields; for they are white already to harvest" (Jn. 4:35b). Reapers watch their fields to know when the crops are ready. A reaper sees when someone wants to be saved.

❀ Listen to God's promptings. As you have been watching and think someone's spiritually ready to be saved, talk to the Lord. Listen to Him with your heart, and you will know when He whispers to you when it's time to reap.

❦ Labor—and then rejoice! Reapers work hard—they can't afford to be lazy come harvest time. The spiritual souls of so many people depend on the reaper's job. When we labor in God's timing, reapers "gathereth fruit unto life eternal: that both he that soweth and he that reapeth may rejoice together" (Jn. 4:36). Reapers don't rejoice alone; they rejoice together with the sowers. While on earth and then later in heaven, we will rejoice at all we have together accomplished for the Lord!

Sowers and reapers, do you see why it's important we work together for the Lord of harvest? God will reward us for everything we did for Him—and we will rejoice!

The Samaritan Woman's Roots and Fruits

Let's not remember the Samaritan Woman for her life of sin. Let's remember her as a great woman missionary who sowed seeds and reaped souls for the Lord! The Lord used her to bring an amazing spiritual revival to her Samaritan village—something Jesus never experienced any other time He lived on the earth. After Jesus' resurrection, more disciples preached in Samaria; they sowed gospel seeds, reaped souls, and planted churches (Acts 8:25, 9:31). The Samaritan Woman's spiritual fruit spread and sprang up throughout her hometown. Look at all that grew from one gospel seed!

How can you grow in the season of sowing and reaping?

Are you sowing seeds and/or reaping souls for the Lord? If so, you are growing in your spiritual life. The Lord uses what you do in these seasons and will "multiply your seed sown, and increase the fruits of your righteousness" (2 Cor. 9:10). He strengthens you as you work for Him and increases what you have done. That's what I call growth! Whether you're a sower, a reaper, or both—you will grow in the Lord as you reach souls for Him.

Digging Deeper

Memorize John 4:36: *"And he that reapeth receiveth wages, and gathereth fruit unto life eternal: that both he that soweth and he that reapeth may rejoice together."*

Branching Out

1. Write down a way you can sow a gospel seed this week.

   _____

   _____

2. How do sowers and reapers work together to reach people to the Lord? _____

   _____

   _____

3. How has this study encouraged you to be a sower and/or a reaper for the Lord?_____

   _____

   _____

4. What does Psalm 126:5-6 promise? _____

   _____

   _____

*I can grow and bear fruit in the seasons of sowing and reaping by*_____

_____

_____

Chapter Eight

Growing in Our Influence to Others

Season: A Grandma

Grandma Lois
Acts 14:6-7, 16:1

My grandma Wilhelm's family gave her a good start for a spiritual legacy. They loved and followed the Lord, and she chose to do the same. She married my grandpa who became a Methodist preacher, a great-grandnephew of Charles Wesley. Grandma supported grandpa as a preacher's wife for 60 plus years of ministry. Each of her four children loves the Lord; two serve in full time ministry and the other two faithfully love their families and church. About 20 from her direct family, including grandchildren and great-grandchildren, serve the Lord as missionaries or preachers. Though she's no longer living, her spiritual influence lives in my heart and many others in our family.

When we influence others, we never know who can be affected by our life—some may never know us and we may never know them. God uses the invisible force of influence in mysterious ways. The word *influence* literally means "a flowing into" and "in a general sense…whose operation is invisible and known only by its effects, or a power whose cause and operation are unseen."[63]

Grandmas, you have a special God-given calling in your life—to leave behind a godly influence. As you influence your family, your life can leave behind a godly heritage for all who come behind you. Grandma Lois helped her daughter bring up Timothy, a man who became a missionary and pastor, and her life influenced the world for Christ.

Influence Your Family to Know the Lord

As a young Jewess, Lois understood the importance to keep the deep-rooted Jewish customs and traditions. The Jewish people lived in their own communities and kept their distance from Gentiles. Lois married a Jewish man, according to custom, and gave birth to a daughter named Eunice. Can you sense Lois' shock and disappointment when her daughter married a Gentile man? (You can imagine the rarity of inter-racial marriages that took place around the first century since it's forbidden to do today.)

Eunice had a baby boy, and Lois loved her grandson and his name Timothy, which means "one who honors God." Acts 16:1 mentions that Timothy was "the son of a certain woman, which was a Jewess, and believed; but his father was a Greek." The phrase *was a Greek* in its imperfect tense "indicates that Timothy's father was perhaps dead."[64] With the loss of Timothy's dad, Lois determined to help Eunice bring up her precious grandson.

Her grandmotherly heart ached every time someone in her community looked down upon her Timothy; both the Jewish and Gentile community considered him to be a half-breed. Little did Grandma Lois realize that God would later use Timothy's unique background to reach both Jews and Gentiles for the Lord.

The small town of Lystra didn't have a synagogue (probably due to its small size), and Lois and Eunice might have tag teamed to homeschool Timothy. Like other Jewish boys, Timothy probably memorized the Torah, the first five books of the Bible, by age 12. "The absence of any indication of the existence of a synagogue makes this devout consistency more noticeable."[65] By the time Timothy reached adulthood, he would have memorized large portions of the Old Testament.

Later the apostle Paul credited Timothy's knowledge of the Scriptures to Grandma Lois and Eunice. He said, "But continue thou in the things which thou hast learned and hast been assured of, knowing of whom thou hast learned them. And that from a child [literally "from an infant"] thou hast known the holy scriptures" (2 Tim. 3:14-15).

Maybe you're in a position like Grandma Lois to raise your grandchildren in your own home or close by. Or maybe you're a long-distance grandma and know you don't have many opportunities to be with them. Either way, your life can influence your family and grandchildren to know the Lord and the Bible. Here are some thoughts to help guide you with your important job:

- Know the spiritual state of each your grandchildren. Do you know who's been saved and baptized? Keep records of their spiritual decisions so you can know how to pray for them. The written information will come in handy and help you keep track of them, especially if you have a large family.

- Love your grandchildren. Show and tell that you love them. Everyone feels loved by different ways, and I recommend you read a book called "The Five Love Languages" by Gary Chapman. In the book you'll discover the five ways people feel loved—words, service, touch, gifts, and quality time. Try to discover, learn, and show them ways to feel loved. For example, if they feel loved by words, write them a note. If they feel loved by acts of service, make them something. (I do this as a mom and teacher and believe me, it works!)

- Pray for them. Do you pray for your grandchildren? Have a prayer list written with their name and needs. Let them know you're their prayer warrior. Ask them what you could specifically pray for in their lives. Try to know what's going on in their lives so you know how to pray for them.

- Show them the Bible's real to you. Text or message them with Scripture that has been a blessing to you. Claim a Bible verse for each of your grandchildren.
- Be a faithful attender to church. If you raise them in your home, take them to church with you. Even if you're a long distance grandma, let them know you attend church. This will encourage them to stay faithful.
- Be wise with how you advise. My friend Sue, a grandma, told me, "It's different with grandchildren. Unasked advice could be unwelcomed advice on their part." If you feel led to give advice, handle it wisely.
- Believe in them. Believe that God has a special plan for them. If you don't believe in them, maybe nobody else ever will. Let them be convinced their grandma cheers for them as their number one fan.

Influence Others by Your Love

Lois' curiosity sparked when two missionaries named Paul and Barnabus arrived in town to preach the good news of Jesus Christ (Acts 14:7). A crowd gathered around them and went into an uproar when Paul healed a crippled man. The townspeople began to worship both missionaries who ran throughout the crowd to explain God's power healed the man.

At this moment, other Jews from the neighboring towns appeared and stirred up the crowd to stone Paul. Then they dragged his beaten body outside the city and left him for dead. "Howbeit, as the disciples stood round about him, he rose up, and came into the city" (Acts 14:20). Paul survived the stoning and even traveled 30 miles the next day to preach in a town called Derbe.

Grandma Lois must have been surprised to see the two missionaries return back to her town (Acts 14:21)! They told the other believers they returned back in order to start a church.

Grandma Lois felt excited to know she and her family would have a place to worship God! At the new church, Paul taught God's Word, strengthened the people's faith, and ordained elders. "Though recently converted, these elders were likely Jews who knew the Scriptures."[66] When Paul and Barnabus left the church to travel and preach the gospel, it was their love for the Lord and others that influenced the people at Lystra to continue in the faith.

Do you want to know the secret to influence? It's love. I am blessed to know many people who live godly lives; however, those who have really influenced—really touched—my life are those who have shown a love for the Lord, for others, and for me. Yes, a good example and a godly testimony add credibility to influence, but love is the source of the power of influence.

Paul's love for the Lord and others gave him influence. He told Christians he loved them "as a nurse cherisheth her children: So being affectionately desirous of you, we were willing to have imparted unto you, not the gospel of God only, but also our own souls, because ye were dear unto us…As ye know how we exhorted and comforted and charged every one of you, as a father doth his children, That ye would walk worthy of God, who hath called you unto his kingdom and glory" (1 Thess. 2:7-8, 11-12). Paul's love encouraged others to grow in the Lord. Do you think his life would have been as influential if he didn't show love?

For your life to influence others, they must see and sense your love. Grandmas, do you love your grandchildren? Do they know you love them? Whether you live close by or long-distance, you can show your family you love them with birthday cards, phone conversations, gifts, and the words "I love you." They will sense your love for them, and you will influence them.

Influence—then Let Go

Three years later, in the year AD 51, an excited Grandma Lois welcomed Paul and Silas, Paul's new Gentile missionary friend, back to town. Paul rejoiced to see Timothy, his "beloved son" (1 Cor. 4:17), and heard many good reports about Timothy (Acts 16:2). Paul invited Timothy to join his missionary team, and Grandma Lois and Eunice felt excited. Maybe they used to wonder if a household of women could train a boy to be a godly man of character; they didn't have to wonder anymore—Paul chose Timothy to be on his team!

Would you allow your child or grandchild to be a traveling companion with someone your community once attempted to kill and left for dead? We can imagine what words and thoughts may have been exchanged between Paul, Grandma Lois, and Eunice.

Paul: "I'd like Timothy to join Silas and me. He has both character and passion for the Lord and His work. His unique family background can also help us reach both Jews and Gentiles."

Grandma Lois and Eunice might have thought this: "Whoa, hold your horses! We know all about the bad things that happen to you—the shipwrecks, the beatings. Timothy could get killed hanging out with you!"

However, I wonder if they said: "Paul, we have brought Timothy up for this very moment—to do what God has called him to do. May Timothy strengthen you, your ministry, and lead many people to the Lord. We leave him in God's hands."

Another ordination ceremony took place at their church (referenced by Paul in 1 Timothy 4:14). This time, the elders laid their hands on and prayed for Timothy! Grandma Lois and Eunice said goodbye to Timothy. They influenced him the best they could and now had to let him go.

It's hard to let go of someone you love. Last December, I had to let go of my nine- year-old daughter Tirzah. She flew on an airplane by herself from Phoenix to Oklahoma to be with her adopted Grandma and Grandpa Hardy. I'll be honest; as we made the plans, I had some butterflies in my stomach about the trip. I hoped and prayed for her safety. The morning before we said goodbye and she left for the airport with her daddy, something wonderful happened in my heart—I felt incredible peace. I felt happy and excited for her that she had this amazing opportunity to go on the trip and be with family. Tirzah loved her time with the Hardys, and they had a godly influence in her life. She returned back home to us with the sweetest spirit, and I was so thankful we had let her go.

Unfortunately, letting go isn't a one-time ordeal; it'll need to happen many times. We need to let our loved ones go when they head to school for the day, work at a job, experience a mission trip, go off to college, get married, and parent their own children. As we let them go, we release our tight grip from them and leave them in God's hands. We can take our empty hands to cling to the Lord and draw our strength from Him.

Whenever we let go of a loved one—whether it's to a mission field or just down the street—we need to commit them to the Lord. We need to pray for them and ask the Lord's blessing on them (1 Chron. 29:19). If you struggle with this, you could pray something like, "Okay, Lord, I need your help! I am letting go of _____ and leaving her/him in your hands." *Letting go is more than just a physical act—it's a spiritual act. It's a peace you have made with the Lord.*

Influence Affects Those Who Walk Behind You

Timothy and Paul traveled many miles for Paul's second journey and continued for a third missionary journey. They helped strengthen other believers and establish churches; many people became saved and baptized. For 13 years they traveled as partners until AD 64 when Timothy became "ordained the first bishop of the church of the Ephesians" (2 Tim. 4:22). Paul wrote Timothy a letter called "First Timothy" to give him advice for his new ministry.

Three years later, Paul wrote Timothy another letter called "Second Timothy." This second letter contained sad news for Timothy. Paul had written it from a dark, damp prison cell and asked Timothy to visit him before Emperor Nero killed him. Paul even made arrangements for a man named Tychicus to "fill in the pulpit" for Timothy at Ephesus. Timothy hurried to gather the coat and books Paul requested and arrived in Rome with his friend Mark.

It saddened Timothy to say his last goodbye to a man who had been like a father to him (1 Cor. 4:17). Timothy grieved when he heard the news of Paul's death. Tradition says Timothy remained in Ephesus for the next 34 years until his death in AD 97.

Psalm 23:6 says, "Surely goodness and mercy shall follow me all the days of my life." Did you know that "goodness and mercy" literally refers to manure dropped from the sheep? As a shepherd would lead his flock down a mountain, the sheep would leave behind them a trail of manure. The shepherd's nickname for his sheep is "golden hooves;"[67] he loves how their droppings enrich the soil of those who follow after them.

I know it's not the cleanest of illustrations, but it really does illustrate influence. Jesus is our Good Shepherd; He prepares and makes available to us things good for us. As I follow the Lord, "goodness and mercy should follow me, should be left behind me, as a legacy to others, wherever I may go."[68]

And this is the beauty of influence—it spreads. You may concentrate your influence on your family members, but it can even touch the lives of those you will never come in contact. One goal every grandma, every Christian woman, should have is to be a godly influence in other people's lives. Sir Alfred Lord Tennyson wrote, "The good men do lives after them."[69] Whose life are you influencing? Will your influence spread to others when you are gone? What kind of legacy will you leave behind for your family and others?

Grandma Lois' Roots and Fruits

Did you know the word *grandmother* is used only once in the Bible? Paul wrote in a letter to Timothy, "I call to remembrance the unfeigned faith that is in thee, *which dwelt first in thy grandmother Lois,* and thy mother Eunice; and I am persuaded that in thee also" (2 Tim. 1:5) (emphasis mine). Grandma Lois' faith started the chain of influence for three generations of her family! Her influence didn't stop with her family—it started. God used Grandma Lois, Eunice, and Timothy to reach many people for Him and His kingdom.

How can you grow in the season of being a grandma?

Do you see the important job God has called you to do? We need godly grandmas in today's age to influence others for the Lord. Your family needs you to be there for them. Whether you're a long-distance grandma or you stay close to home, you should have the same goal—to influence your family to know and grow in the Lord. May the Lord help you to leave behind, to drop, for your family tree a spiritual heritage!

Digging Deeper

Memorize Psalm 23:6: *"Surely goodness and mercy shall follow me all the days of my life: and I will dwell in the house of the LORD for ever."*

Branching Out

1. Are you a negative or positive influence in your family for the Lord? _____

   _____

   _____

2. Is there someone in your family you need to let go and entrust them in God's hands? Pray and ask the Lord to help you do this. _____

   _____

   _____

3. Think of someone in your family who would needs to hear from you. Write them a letter, email, send a text, or call them to encourage in the Lord. _____

   _____

   _____

4. How can you be a godly influence in your family?

   _____

   _____

I can grow and bear fruit as a grandma by_____

_____

_____

Chapter Nine

Growing in Compassion with Action

Season: Caregiver

Nurse Deborah and
Midwives Shiphrah and Puah

A little girl wondered how she could nurse her sick mother back to health. One day, after she helped settle her mother comfortably in bed, the little girl slipped into the kitchen. She had seen her mother make hot tea for her father when he was sick and decided to do the same for her ailing mom. With cup and saucer in hand, she took the tea into the bedroom. The mother, touched by this sweet act of compassion, praised her daughter and said, "I didn't know you could make tea."

The little girl beamed with pride as she told her mom how she made it. She explained, "I boiled the water and tea leaves together just like you always do." The mother listened attentively while sipping the tea. The girl continued her story by stating, "But I couldn't find the little strainer thing so I used the fly-swatter." Her mom nearly spit out the tea as she exclaimed, "You used the fly-swatter!" The little girl comforted her mother's concerns by explaining, "Oh, but don't worry, Mommy. I used the old fly-swatter so I wouldn't mess up the new one."[70]

Doesn't the little girl's compassion make your heart smile and your lips chuckle? Compassion, which means "to suffer with," is a mixture of love and sorrow that produces an action. More than seeing someone in need, it's taking action to care for those needs. When others see our heart of compassion, they will see God's love in our life. Do you want others to see and embrace God's love? Your life of compassion can turn their eyes to the Lord (I John 3:17).

When you hear the word *caregiver* today, lots of thoughts can pop into our head: nurses, moms, dads, grandmas, grandpas, foster parents, children taking care of parents, nursery workers, and babysitters (and the list goes on!). You are a caregiver if you take care of someone else's needs. In Bible times, a caregiver was called a nurse, someone who helped nurture growth in another person. Three examples of compassionate caregivers from the Bible are Deborah, Shiphrah and Puah. The compassion these women had will move your heart—and hopefully your body into action!

Compassion has Action
Deborah—Genesis 24:15-67, 35:8

Deborah lived in the land of Mesopotamia, the country of Turkey today, with a family that employed her as the family nurse. Her job consisted of being a nanny, or a second mother, to a spunky girl named Rebekah and her rambunctious brother Laban. Deborah's boss Bethuel was the head of the family and provided for his household plenty of "straw and provender enough, and room to lodge in" (Gen. 24:25).

Deborah watched Rebekah blossom into a beautiful woman and knew it to be a matter of time before some smart, handsome young man would want to marry her. When Rebekah came home one afternoon wearing beautiful jewelry, Deborah listened as Rebekah shared an amazing encounter she just had with an older man by a well.

Look at my new earring and bracelets! You'll never believe what happened to me today when I went to the well. An older man—a stranger from some far away land—asked me to get him some water with my pot from the well. The poor man looked so tired and thirsty;

I hurried to give him water and also his 10 camels. After I did, he approached me with this jewelry and asked me about my family. I told him I was Bethuel's daughter and that my grandparents were Nahor and Milcah. I invited him to stay with us tonight and then he did something unusual—he bowed his head and, I believe, talked to God!

Everyone marveled at Rebekah's story and the household prepared to accommodate the stranger, his servants, and camels. After Laban greeted the man, the servant introduced himself as Abraham's servant. Excitement rang through the whole family to hear the servant bring news of Abraham (Bethuel's uncle) and their long distance relatives. The servant shared how Abraham appointed him to find a wife for Isaac, and how God providentially arranged for Rebekah to be the match. An excited Rebekah, along with her family, accepted the marriage proposal and prepared to pack for the journey.

Deborah also packed her own bags. "And they sent away Rebekah their sister, and her nurse [Deborah]" (Gen. 24:59). Other servants attended Rebekah on the long 500 mile trip (Gen. 24:61), but Deborah had the privilege to be a personal nurse—and second mother—to Rebekah. When the long journey ended, Deborah felt excited to be part of her new family.

Deborah's compassion moved her to action—literally! Sympathy feels another person's suffering, and compassion takes that feeling to the next level. Compassion feels someone's suffering and wants to help them. There's action with compassion. **Every** time Jesus had compassion for either one person or a group of people, He acted.

Every one of us caregivers should want to be compassionate. For me, compassion doesn't come naturally; it's an area in which I strive to grow. Maybe you're different and know that compassion is your spiritual passion. Despite how we're wired, we all need to have compassion. Especially if we are caregivers! Here are some ways we can be compassionate—

Be there for someone else. You may wonder sometimes how you can show care to someone in need. Did you know your physical presence can show compassion? When you are there for someone in need, you send them a quiet message that says, "I feel your pain; I'm here for you." We are God's hands, feet, mouth, and ears for those He wants to touch. If you can't physically be there for someone, call them. Send a card. Let them know that you will be there for them emotionally.

Use the personality and gifts God gave you to bless others. Compassionate women aren't just the soft, quiet type. Every women of every personality needs to grow in compassion. Use the gifts God gave you. If you like to cook, make a meal; if you like to give, buy a meal or slip some money into a card; if you like to sit and listen, your presence would bring comfort. Maybe you would like to clean someone's house (come on over to mine!); go for it! Use the personality and grace the Lord gives you to be a blessing and take action!

Compassion Goes Above and Beyond the Call of Duty

For the next 97 years, Deborah eye witnessed many household changes: Rebekah struggled with infertility for 20 years, her twin boys Jacob and Esau constantly competed, Esau married worldly women, Isaac accumulated wealth, and Jacob deceived his father and stole his brother's blessing. Jacob was probably her favorite boy since he was Rebekah's, and Deborah felt sad the day he ran away to escape Esau's anger.

Loyal Deborah stayed with Rebekah to be a caregiver for Isaac who, by this time, was blind and 137 years old. It must have been a shock and grief to Deborah when Rebekah died first. Later, Deborah joined to Jacob's family of four wives and 13 children (either before or after Jacob's move to the land of Canaan). The roles reversed— Deborah was now a very old woman, and Jacob's family helped take care of her.

When God ordered Jacob to move his family to Bethel (Gen. 35:1), Deborah was around 170 years old.[71] After Jacob built an altar and worshipped the Lord, she died. Jacob buried her body underneath an oak tree and "the name of it was called Allon-bachuth" (Gen. 35:8), which means "oak of weeping."[72] The tears the family shed over her death and the beautiful memorial reveal their love for their beloved nurse. Her death was more than a servant's death; servants died unnoticed, but "the special attention given Deborah at her death is unusual."[73] Her death was more like that of a family member, and her compassion went far above and beyond her call of duty.

If you're a caregiver, you know what it's like to feel duty towards someone else. It's good to have a sense of duty towards someone, yet compassion goes a step further. Compassion goes above and beyond the call of duty.

Honestly, it's hard sometimes to be compassionate, and it can be even harder to meet the needs of some who might be cranky or ungrateful. The struggle is real! This is when we need to think of the Lord and His compassion for us. I am so thankful the Lord went above and beyond His call of duty when He died on the cross for me—not out of duty but because of His compassion.

As you look through the chart on the next page, ask yourself if what you do for others comes from duty or a heart of compassion.

Duty	vs.	Compassion
Something you have to do		Something you want to do
Views people as a job		Views people as opportunities to show and give God's love
Takes care of person's basic physical needs		Meets extra physical needs along with emotional and spiritual needs
May go out of way if it feels other person deserves it		Goes out of way for anyone— even someone grouchy, unlovable, and undeserving
Goal is to survive by the end of the day		Goal is to bring comfort and hope to others
Reward comes from paycheck		Reward comes as we nurture, encourage, and comfort

Compassion's Strength Comes from the Lord
Shiphrah and Puah—Ex.1:15-22

Shiphrah and Puah heard their family tell stories of a time when Jews and Egyptians lived in peace. They would cheer when they heard how God used Joseph, a Jewish man who became an Egyptian Pharaoh, to save the Jewish people; he gave his family land in Egypt, a fertile land watered by the Nile River, to live during a severe time of famine. Three hundred years later, the Israelites still lived in Goshen and "were fruitful, and increased abundantly, and multiplied, and waxed exceeding mighty; and the land was filled with them" (Ex. 1:7).

"Now there arose up a new king over Egypt, which knew not Joseph" (Ex. 1:8). Maybe this other king came from a different land and conquered Egypt.[74] With the hostile change in attitude the Egyptians had toward the Israelites, Shiphrah and Puah were no longer free; they were slaves. The new Pharaoh reminded them of their new slave status when he "set over them taskmasters to afflict them with their burdens" (Ex.1:11). Days of peace became a distant memory to the Israelites, and some even turned to Egyptian idols to bring them comfort (Josh. 24:14).

Shiphrah and Puah served many Jewish women in a needful way—they were midwives. The Jewish women loved having children, and Shiphrah and Puah probably had hundreds of Hebrew women clients. "Aben Ezra, the ancient Jewish historian, says that these two women 'were chiefs over all the midwives, who were more than 500.'"[75]

Pharaoh summoned the two midwives before him, and "he said, When ye do the office of a midwife to the Hebrew women, and see them upon the stools; it if be a son, then ye shall kill him: but if it be a daughter, then she shall live. But the midwives feared God, and did not as the king of Egypt commanded them, but saved the men children alive" (Ex. 1:16-17).

Whispers of Pharaoh's command spread to every Jewish home in the land of Goshen. Shiphrah and Puah encouraged all the midwives to disobey the Pharaoh's orders in order to save the lives of the babies. Because they risked their own lives to keep their Jewish people alive, God gave them the strength they needed for compassion.

Compassion comes from God along with His strength for compassion. When God had compassion on us and sent Jesus to die for us, His compassion gave Jesus strength to have compassion towards us. "Who comforteth us in all our tribulation, that we may be able to comfort them which are in any trouble, by the comfort wherewith we ourselves are comforted of God" (2 Cor. 1:4). Jesus gave His life for us; we, too, should be willing to make smaller sacrifices which can help others in their distress.[76]

Sometimes, though, we try to muster up compassion in our own strength and then get burned out. Have you ever heard of "compassion fatigue"? A common condition that caregivers get, it slows down and sometimes stops any compassion they might feel. Since we need to grow, not shrink, in our compassion, we'll need to use the Lord's strength to be our compassion.

As the Lord strengthens our compassion, we have the opportunity to show others His compassion. First John 3:17 says, "But whoso hath this world's good, and seeth his brother have need, and shutteth up his bowels of compassion from him, how dwelleth the love of God in him?" If we flip it around, it could say something like this, "If we see somebody in need and have compassion on them, they will see God's love in us." Let's use God's strength and compassion to be a powerful testimony and lead people to Him!

Compassion Blesses Others Physically and Spiritually

Shiphrah and Puah stood before Pharaoh the second time. He growled, "Why have ye done this thing, and have saved the men children alive? And the midwives said unto Pharaoh, Because the Hebrew women are not as the Egyptian women; for they are lively, and are delivered ere the midwives come in unto them" (Ex. 1:18-19).

Maybe they lied to Pharaoh, or maybe they told the truth. It is possible God did intervene in a miraculous way with the birthing of the babies. "It is plain that the Hebrews were now under an extraordinary blessing of increase…that the women had very quick and easy labour… they seldom needed the help of midwives: this the midwives took notice of, and, concluding it to be the finger of God, were thereby emboldened to disobey the king…and with this justified themselves before Pharaoh, when he called them to an account for it."[77]

Pharaoh actually believed the women and accepted their excuse! (That was another miracle!) "Therefore God dealt well with the midwives: and the people multiplied, and waxed very mighty. And it came to pass, because the midwives feared God, that he made them houses" (Ex. 1:20-21). Look at how God blessed them and their people for their obedience and compassion!

Our compassion can bless others physically. I remember the birth of each of my children and the sobering reality of how much their life depended on me. As birthdays roll around each year, I celebrate with them their life. I thank the Lord He gave them to me to take care of and to be a part of their growth. Being a caregiver is an important job. Others depend on you for their growth and quality of life. Your life plays a huge role to physically develop those entrusted in your care.

Our compassion can bless others spiritually. Did you know that your compassion can lead someone to the Lord? Jude 22 says, "And of some have compassion, making a difference." This verse literally talks about how some people come to know the Lord because someone else had compassion on them. When people see our compassion for them, they will see God's love for them as well. Our compassion with action can literally affect someone to take spiritual action.

The late Colonel Sanders (of Kentucky Fried Chicken) was on an airplane when an infant screamed nonstop. The mother and flight attendants tried every trick to quiet the baby. Finally, the Colonel asked if he could hold the baby. He gently rocked it to sleep. Later a passenger said, "We all appreciate what you did for us." Colonel Sanders replied, "I didn't do it for us; I did it for the baby." Such a beautiful picture of compassion! Our motives behind compassion should always be pure and selfless. And when we take action to meet someone else's needs, our compassion will be a blessing to so many others!

Deborah's, Shiphrah and Puah's Fruits and Roots

Deborah was an ordinary nurse who served in a dysfunctional family with a history of swindling, polygamy, murder, rape, jealousy and betrayal. And yet, everyone wept at her passing because her roots of compassion reached out to the entire family. Her heart of compassion touched so many other hearts.

Shiphrah and Puah's fear of the Lord compelled them to show compassion on the boy babies. And though we don't know exactly how, their courage must have influenced other midwives to trust in the Lord. Their compassion literally saved an entire nation from extinction!

How can you grow in compassion in your season of caregiving?

Though God's compassion is full (Ps. 86:15), He renews His compassion "every morning" (Lam. 3:23) and gives it to us for our day. His compassion has a cycle, a growth. In the same way, though our compassion will never be full and perfect like His, we can renew our compassion every morning with the Lord's strength to liberally give to others throughout the day. This gives our compassion freshness, a growth. The more we give our compassion, the more we will grow in compassion.

Digging Deeper

Memorize First John 3:17: *"But whoso hath this world's good, and seeth his brother have need, and shutteth up his bowels of compassion from him, how dwelleth the love of God in him?"*

Branching Out

1. Based on Matthew 18:33, why should the Lord's compassion compel you to be compassionate? _____

_____

_____

2. How can you use your personality strengths to be
   compassionate? _____

   _____

   _____

3. In Luke 10:29-37, how did the Good Samaritan show action to
   his compassion? What did Jesus say we are to do to others in
   verse 37? _____

4. _____

   _____

5. How can you show compassion this week? _____

   _____

   _____

I can grow and bear fruit as a caregiver by_____

_____

_____

Chapter Ten

Growing in Grace

In Every Season of Life

Anna
Luke 2:36-38

A family adopted an eight year old girl they didn't love. Every time they took a family vacation to Disneyland, they left the little girl at a friend's house. Eventually the parents dissolved the adoption, and another family adopted the little girl. When the new adoptive parents heard her story about Disneyland, they made arrangements to go there with her. The little girl felt excited to finally go to Disneyland, but deep in her heart she wondered if they would really take her. The month before vacation time, her attitude and behavior took a turn for the worst.

A few days before the trip, the father pulled the little girl aside to have a little talk. "I know what you're going to do," she stated flatly. "You're not going to take me to Disneyland, are you?" The thought never crossed the dad's mind; he just wanted to encourage her to have better behavior. He tried to assure her that since she was part of the family, she would be going to Disneyland.

The girl's bad attitude vanished by the end of the first night at Disneyland. The father asked her how she enjoyed her day. "Daddy," she said, "I finally got to go to Disneyland. But it wasn't because I was good; it's because I'm yours."[78]

What a beautiful picture of grace! The Lord gives us grace, not because of who we are but because of who He is. Grace comes from the love and gifts of our Father. Grace is God's divine, favorable influence in our life; it's a supernatural ability the Lord gives us to do something for Him. Our first embrace of grace comes when we ask Christ to be our Savior. But grace is more than just a one-time event—it's also for today.

Christian growth begins by grace and continues with grace; we are encouraged to grow in grace (2 Pet. 3:18). Anna, a woman of "great age" (Luke 2:36), grew in grace. With a name that means "grace," Anna spent her entire life in devotion and service to the Lord. While she waited in constant expectation for the coming of the Messiah, she used God's grace for His work. Through His grace, she gave back to the Lord lots of glory.

The Grace Gifts

Before Jesus' earthly birth, spiritual silence hovered over the land of Israel (Luke 1:79). The spirit of prophecy the Jews experienced four hundred years earlier ceased, and the people established their own religious system. Their high priest should have come from the line of Aaron; instead, they allowed King Herod the Great, the ruler of the Jews, to pick their High Priest. Their religious leaders would "curry favor with the wicked Herod, overlook his evils, and encourage and influence the other priests to do likewise—all of which would corrupt the priesthood in a great way."[79]

In the midst of the spiritual darkness, a small group of people—a remnant—remained faithful to the Lord. Anna was part of the remnant. "And there was one Anna, a prophetess, the daughter of Phanuel, of the tribe of Aser [Asher]" (Luke 2:36). Anna's father's name Phanuel means "the face or appearance of God,"[80] and Anna longed to see the face of God, the Messiah who prophets predicted would come and deliver the Jews..

By Anna's time, most Jews didn't know from which tribe of Israel they came. Anna knew her family's heritage traced back to the tribe of Asher. About 700 years earlier, in 722 BC, the Assyrians kidnapped the people of her tribe along with nine other tribes (called the ten lost tribes of Israel). Good families later migrated south to Jerusalem to be near the temple and worship the Lord. If the family never preserved its family tree records, most Jews claimed to be from the tribe of Benjamin or Judah.[81] Eight centuries later, Anna's family "had not failed to keep a record of the heritage. All of this shows the devotion of the family of God. No wonder Anna was the godly woman she was; she had a good heritage."[82]

As a prophetess, her ministry included duties of teaching and speaking. If she received any divine revelations, none are recorded. "Perhaps…she was the one who had understanding in the scriptures above other women, and made it her business to instruct the younger women in the things of God."[83] Especially during a corrupt religious system, other women needed Anna's unique ministry to help them know and grow in the Lord. Anna used God's gifts of grace to help her through her time of heartache and then her ministry to the Lord and others.

Do you want to do something for the Lord? You can, by God's grace. Do you ever think, "I would like to do _____ for the Lord but I don't have the_____." You can, by God's grace. God gives us grace—His favor, power, and resources—so we will do things for Him. I call these "grace gifts." Hopefully the check marks below will help you understand about "grace gifts" and how they work.

🌸 God gives you grace
🌸 You accept His grace
🌸 You use His grace through Him then for Him

We should never use our "grace gifts" for our own personal goals and glory; that would make His grace in us useless or vain. "But by the grace of God I am what I am: and his grace which was bestowed upon me was not in vain; but I laboured more abundantly

103

than they all: yet not I, but the grace of God which was with me" (1 Cor. 15:10).

Grace is the gift that keeps on giving. As you grow in grace, your "grace gifts" can keep going and going –like that energizer bunny commercial from the 80's. The secret to keep your "grace gifts" going and going is to use them by God's grace and then for Him.

The Growth of Grace

Anna "was of a great age, and had lived with an husband seven years from her virginity; And she was a widow of about fourscore and four years" (Luke 2:36-37). Since the average Jewish teenage girl married around 13 years old, Anna could have been a widow around 20 years old. Along with the loss of her husband, it must have been another sting of reproach to remain childless.

Anna prayed and sought the Lord's will and direction for her life. She knew widows didn't have any way of support; many lived with their children or returned back home to live with their father's house. Originally, God had set in place laws for the Jews to take care of their widows (Deut. 24:19-21); unfortunately, by Anna's time, the religious system took advantage of the widows.

Anna wanted to be closer to God and decided to spend her time at the temple. "She did not bury her hope in a grave. In the place of what God took, He gave her more of Himself, and she became devoted to him who had been promised to be as a Husband to the widow, and through her long widowhood was unwearying in devotion to Him."[84]

She "departed not from the temple" (Luke 2:37). It's unclear whether she spent most of her time during the day at the temple and then went home, or if she literally lived on the temple grounds. Anna could have lived in a little apartment called a portico, the housing where the priests would temporarily live to fulfill their priestly duties in Jerusalem.[85]

Anna "served God with fastings and prayers night and day" (Luke 2:37). Wow—she fasted and prayed *day and night*! That's an incredible prayer life for a little old lady—actually, for any kind of lady! From her life we can see that as she grew in her relationship with the Lord, she grew in grace.

Who can grow in grace? Anybody who has accepted Jesus as their Savior can grow in grace. Did you know children should be growing in grace? Jesus grew in grace when He was a child (Luke 2:40). From children to super senior saints, we need to grow in grace in every season of life.

What does it mean to grow in grace? It's when we "increase in the image and favor of God."[86] Second Peter 3:18 say, "But grow in grace, and in the knowledge of our Lord and Savior Jesus Christ. To him be glory both now and for ever." In order to grow in grace, we need to strengthen our personal relationship with the Lord. The more we know about the Lord, the more we grow in grace. The more we grow in grace, the more we bring glory Him.

For example, I am short and my husband Tim is tall. Imagine that Tim and I are both in the kitchen and I need to reach something from the tippy-top cupboard. I could ask Tim for help but then decide not to. Instead, I rush out the front door and run to the end of the street. I knock on our neighborhood policeman's door and ask him for help. Wouldn't that be kind of silly? I know how my husband would feel about that!

I know it sounds unrealistic, but in reality it's what we have done to the Lord at times. God lives inside us; He offers us His grace. Instead of growing in grace, we reject His help and run around to do things in our own strength. To grow in grace, we first need to acknowledge God's presence and power. Second, we need to place all our dependence upon Him and His supernatural strength. As we grow in grace, He enables us to grasp those things far away from our reach.

The Cycle of Grace

One day, while Anna served in her daily ministries at the temple, she spotted her elderly friend Simeon with a couple and a newborn baby. Also part of the remnant, Simeon prophesied that the baby would bring salvation to the world. "In that instant" (God's providential timing in Luke 2:38), Anna joined the group and with her aged eyesight beheld the Messiah! Can you visualize her tender admiration for baby Jesus, the son of God? "Anna's great dedication to God resulted in her being in the Temple when Christ came to the Temple. Had she not been so dedicated, she would have missed the greatest of blessings."[87]

Immediately she "gave thanks likewise unto the Lord, and spake of him to all them that looked for redemption in Jerusalem" (Luke 2:38). For a little old lady, she moved fast! She ran around, found those in her remnant group, and told them about Jesus. People knew if anybody witnessed the mind and heart of God, it was Anna. As she shared with others her eyewitness of the Lord, her testimony gave the Lord lots of glory.

Do you tell others about the Lord's glory? We can't assume that people will look at our grace-filled life and give God glory. Some people honestly wonder how we do the things we do. This can be a great time to witness to someone about salvation through Jesus or the power He gives in our Christian lives. Whether it's a compliment on a song we sang, a lesson we taught, a friendship restored, or our consistent service to the Lord, it's a perfect opportunity for us to share with others all the Lord has done for us and give Him the glory.

Do others see God's glory in your life? The ultimate goal of every Christian woman should be for her life to bring honor and glory to the Lord. It's so easy to take credit for what we accomplish, yet we need to realize that without the Lord we can do nothing. "That the name of our Lord Jesus Christ may be glorified in you, and ye in him, according to the grace of our God and the Lord Jesus Christ" (2 Thess. 1:12).

Giving glory to the Lord completes our cycle of grace. After you give Him glory, you can start your "grace gifts" cycle all over again!

- God gives us grace
- We accept His grace
- We use His grace through Him then for Him
- He gets glory from our grace

Let's give God lots of glory since He gives us lots of grace!

The Cost of Grace

Later, when Anna returned to her room, I'm sure she again thanked the Lord for the opportunity to see the Messiah. Surely she felt God's grace, His favor, shine on her. All her self-denial, personal sacrifices, and service in the ministry had just been rewarded by Him. I believe Anna felt "ready to depart in peace and be joined with her husband above."[88]

The arrival of Jesus changed the spiritual course of the world. Up until His death, the people lived during a time called the old covenant, a time that emphasized the laws given by Moses and the priesthood. When Jesus sacrificed His life on the cross for us, He became our high priest (Heb. 8:3). After His resurrection, a new time called the new covenant became established. In our new covenant, or testament, we now can be saved by grace through our faith in Jesus Christ (Eph. 2:8). We now live in the age of grace.

"But we see Jesus...that he by the grace of God should taste death for every man" (Heb. 2:9). Do you see the cost of our grace? It cost our Lord His life. I'm so thankful we don't have to pay a price for grace since Jesus paid ours on the cross. Grace might be free to us, but it wasn't free to Him. There would be no grace if Jesus didn't pay a cost. His death and life gives us grace.

Don't you value a gift when you realize someone puts a lot of time, energy, and sacrifice into it? When my daughter Tirzah was in the third grade, for Christmas she presented to me a small, crinkly looking gift with bows taped all over it. Inside the wrapping paper was a card. I opened it up to find 27 dollars on the inside (made up of a five dollar bill and the rest ones) and a handwritten note. It said, (and I quote): *"Dear, Mama I don't relly know how to put it but I know your going to like it. I'm geting you a day away from the kids all the kids are going to a friend's house. Jan 19. P.s. with the mony buy wetever you want. Love, Tirzah."*

Awwww! Tirzah made arrangements with three other moms to watch my four kids so I could have a night and day away! When the Friday afternoon rolled around, I did drop the other three kids off at their places. Before I dropped Tirzah off, we spent time together and ate a fun lunch topped off with candy bars. I wanted to show her I really appreciated her special gift. I knew how much it cost her.

Do you want to grow in grace? You'll need to understand the cost for your grace. As we appreciate the Lord's88 sacrifice to give us grace, we will value and treasure our gifts of grace. He sacrificed so much for us to have grace. Aren't you so thankful for all God's grace? Are you using His "grace gifts" so you can give back to Him lots of glory?

Anna's Roots and Fruits

When you think of Anna, do you think of a life full of heartaches and struggles, or a life full of God's grace and glory? Anna's life and beautiful testimony shows us how growing in God's grace can change our tears to joy and our personal loss to personal growth.

Though she never left behind a physical heritage, she did pass on a great spiritual heritage. Her amazing sixty four year record of service to the Lord and personal self-denial reveal her to be the most spiritually devoted woman mentioned in the Bible. Did you know Anna became the first woman missionary to tell others about Jesus? Wow—she really used her "grace gifts" and brought lots of glory to the Lord!

How can you grow in grace in every season?

By now I hope you understand that grace truly is a gift from God; it's not something we can work for and try to earn. We don't gain grace by our good works; our good works come as a product from His grace. When God does give us our "grace gifts," we use His grace for His work. Then we give Him glory. As we continue our cycle of "grace gifts," we will experience growth in our grace. In every season of life, we can grow in grace when it's all about the Lord and for His glory.

Digging Deeper

Memorize Second Thessalonians 1:12: *"That the name of our Lord Jesus Christ may be glorified in you, and ye in him, according to the grace of our God and the Lord Jesus Christ."*

Branching Out

1. Write out how you can grow in grace. _____

_____

_____

2. What are some "grace gifts" the Lord has given to you that you need to use for Him? _____

_____

_____

3. According to Titus 2:11-12, how should we live when we have God's grace in our life?_____

_____

4. How can you use your "grace gifts" to give glory to the Lord?

_____

_____

I can grow in grace in every season of life by_____

_____

_____

Final Thoughts

Wow! We learned a lot about growing in every season of life, didn't we? I know I did! Thank you for joining me on this journey of growth. I know growing in our life seasons will be full of challenges and pain, but they also come with a purpose and beauty. It really will be worth it all when we reach our last season and have spiritual fruit on our account. Let's keep going and

Growing in Every Season of Life!

[1] Gien Karssen, *Her Name is Woman*, vol. 2 (Colorado Springs, CO: Navpress, 1977), pp. 228-229.

[2] Wikipedia, "Appian Way," published on Sept. 2013, *www.wickipedia.org.*, Oct. 2015.

[3] Charles Ryrie, *Ryrie Study Bible* (Chicago: Moody Publishers, 1994), p. 1693.

[4] Herbert Lockyer, *All the Women of the Bible* (Grand Rapids, MI: Zondervan, 1967), p. 121.

[5] Ibid.

[6] John MacArthur, "Was Phoebe a Deaconess?" Romans 16, *www.gty.org*, Dec. 28, 2015.

[7] John G. Butler, *Paul* (Clinton, Iowa: LBC Publications, 1995), p. 334.

[8] Matthew Henry, *Matthew Henry's Whole Bible Commentary*, Luke 2:40 (Sword Searcher, version 5.5.1.3) [Computer Software]. Broken Arrow, OK: StudyLamp Software LLC, 1995-2009.

[9] Herbert Lockyer, *All the Women of the Bible*, p. 46.

[10] Charles Ryrie, *Ryrie Study Bible*, p. 1653.

[11] Matthew Henry, *Matthew Henry's Whole Bible Commentary*, Luke 2:40 (Sword Searcher, version 5.5.1.3) [Computer Software]. Broken Arrow, OK: StudyLamp Software LLC, 1995-2009.

[12] Herbert Lockyer, *All the Women of the Bible* (Grand Rapids, MI: Zondervan, 1967), p. 46.

[13] Andrew Murray, *The Secrets of the Vine, www.thetransformedsoul.com,* The Transformed Soul: "Abiding and Bearing Fruit" by Dr. D. W. Eckstrand, accessed September 2016.

[14] John G. Butler, *Elisha* (Clinton, Iowa: LBC Publications, 1994), p. 186.

[15] J. Warner Wallace, *"Are Young People Really Leaving Christianity?" www. coldcasechristianity.com, Feb.18, 2015.*

[16] Ibid.

[17] Ibid., p. 192.

[18] Ibid., p. 199.

[19] Ibid., pp. 202-203.

[20] Ralph Waldo Emerson, *www.goodreads.com/quotes*, accessed October 2016.

[21] John G. Butler, *Jesus Christ: His Miracles* (Clinton, Iowa: LBC Publications, 2001), pp. 368-369.

[22] Ibid.

[23] *Pulpit Commentary*, Eph. 3:12 (Sword Searcher, version 5.5.1.3) [Computer Software]. Broken Arrow, OK: StudyLamp Software LLC, 1995-2009.

[24] John G. Butler, *Jesus Christ: His Miracles*, p. 370.

[25] Ibid., p. 372.

[26] *Pulpit Commentary*, Eph. 3:12.

[27] Ibid.

[28] Ibid.

[29] Eusebius, Eusebius of Caesarea on Ancient Images, Book 6 chapter 18, *https://energeticprocession.word, June 2016.*

[30] Google quote for marriage, *http://www.marriage.com.*, Feb. 2016.

[31] John MacArthur, "Experiencing the Power of Christ" Ephesians 3:14-21, *www.gty.org*, Sept. 5, 1993.

[32] John G. Butler, *Moses* (Clinton, Iowa: LBC Publications, 1996), p. 77.

[33] Ibid., p. 160.

[34] *Pulpit Commentary*, Exodus 4:25 (Sword Searcher, version 5.5.1.3) [Computer Software]. Broken Arrow, OK: StudyLamp Software LLC, 1995-2009.

[35] Joe Stowell, *Our Daily Bread*, 2 Cor. 4:8, *www.odb.org*, March 7, 2015.

[36] *https://www.templeinstitute.org/main.htm*, The Temple Institute, Nov. 2015.

[37] International Standard Bible Encyclopedia, Eph. 3:16 (Sword Searcher, version 5.5.1.3) [Computer Software]. Broken Arrow, OK: StudyLamp Software LLC, 1995-2009.

[38] Matthew Henry, *Matthew Henry's Whole Bible Commentary*, 1 Sam. 4:22 (Sword Searcher, version 5.5.1.3) [Computer Software]. Broken Arrow, OK: StudyLamp Software LLC, 1995-2009.

[39] Herbert Lockyer, *All the Women of the Bible* (Grand Rapids, MI: Zondervan, 1967), p. 189.

[40] Shirley Starr, *Women of the Bible: Helpless and Hurting, vol. 3* (Kearney, NE: Morris Publishing, 2004), p. 47.

[41] Charles Ryrie, *Ryrie Study Bible* (Chicago: Moody Publishers, 1994), p. 488.

[42] Google, definition of "identity crisis," *www.google.com/search*, Oct. 2015.

[43] *Pulpit Commentary*, Second Samuel 21:10, (Sword Searcher, version 5.5.1.3) [Computer Software]. Broken Arrow, OK: StudyLamp Software LLC, 1995-2009.

[44] Ibid.

[45] Paul Chappell, *http://ministry127.com*, June 2016.

[46] Biblical Illustrator, (Sword Searcher, version 5.5.1.3) [Computer Software]. Broken Arrow, OK: StudyLamp Software LLC, 1995-2009.

[47] *http://www.livescience.com/656-surprise-rainforest-grows-dry*, June 2016.

[48] Gien Karssen, *Her Name is Woman, Book 2* (Colorado Springs, CO: Navpress, 1977), p. 199.

[49] John MacArthur, "Fishing for Men," Matthew 4:18-22, *www.gty.org*, July 9, 1978.

[50] John MacArthur, *Twelve Ordinary Men* (Nashville, TN: Nelson Books, 2002), p. 90.

[51] Ibid., p. 80.

[52] Ibid., p. 97.

[53] Herbert Lockyer, *All the Women of the Bible* (Grand Rapids, MI: Zondervan, 1967), p. 151.

[54] Gien Karssen, *Her Name is Woman*, p. 197.

[55] Herbert Lockyer, *All the Women of the Bible*, p. 151.

[56] John MacArthur, *Twelve Ordinary Men*, p. 93.

[57] Jim Elliot, *www.brainyquote.com/quotes/quotes/j/jimelliot189251.html*, May 2016.

[58] Elisabeth Elliot, "What are arrows for but to shoot?" by Jim Elliot, *https://tollelege.wordpress.com*, Jan. 10, 2014.

[59] Ibid., 95.

[60] John MacArthur, "Messiah: The Living Water, Part 1," John 4:1-15, *www.gty.com.*, April 21, 2013.

[61] *Eastons Bible Dictionary* (Sword Searcher, version 5.5.1.3) [Computer Software]. Broken Arrow, OK: StudyLamp Software LLC, 1995-2009.

[62] John G. Butler, *Jesus Christ: His Encounters* (Clinton, Iowa: LBC Publications, 2003), p. 98.

[63] *Websters 1828* (Sword Searcher, version 5.5.1.3) [Computer Software]. Broken Arrow, OK: StudyLamp Software LLC, 1995-2009.

[64] John MacArthur, "Evangelism the Right Way," Acts 15:36-16:10, *www.gty.org*, Sept. 23, 1973.

[65] *Pulpit Commentary*, (Sword Searcher, version 5.5.1.3) [Computer Software]. Broken Arrow, OK: StudyLamp Software LLC, 1995-2009.

[66] Charles Ryrie, *Ryrie Study Bible* (Chicago: Moody Publishers, 1994), p.1663.

[67] Phillip Keller, *A Shepherd Looks at Psalm 23* (Minneapolis, MN: World Wide Publications, 1970), p. 131.

[68] Ibid., pp. 130-131.

[69] Phillip Keller, *A Shepherd Looks at Psalm 23*, p. 132.

[70] Unknown source, "Compassion," Striving Together Publications, *www.ministry127*, accessed July 2016.

[71] John G. Butler, *Jacob* (Clinton, Iowa: LBC Publications, 1999), p. 302.

[72] Charles Ryrie, *Ryrie Study Bible* (Chicago: Moody Publishers, 1994), p. 61.

[73] Ibid., p. 308.

[74] John G. Butler, *Moses* (Clinton, Iowa: LBC Publications, 1996), p. 20.

[75] Herbert Lockyer, *All the Women of the Bible* (Grand Rapids, MI: Zondervan, 1967), p. 126.

[76] Albert Barnes, 1 John 3:17 (Sword Searcher, version 5.5.1.3) [Computer Software]. Broken Arrow, OK: StudyLamp Software LLC, 1995-2009.

[77] *MHWBC*, Ex.1:22 (Sword Searcher, version 5.5.1.3) [Computer Software]. Broken Arrow, OK: StudyLamp Software LLC, 1995-2009.

[78] The Perfect Illustration for God's Outrageous Grace, http://zondervanacademic.com, Jeremy Bouma, August 14, 2014.

[79] John MacArthur, *Grace to You*, sermon on Luke 2:36-38, "Testifying to Jesus: Anna," www.gty.org (accessed 2015).

[80] Ibid.

[81] Pulpit commentary, Luke 2:36, (Sword Searcher, version 5.5.1.3) [Computer Software]. Broken Arrow, OK: StudyLamp Software LLC, 1995-2009.

[82] John G. Butler, *Jesus Christ: His Incarnation* (Clinton, Iowa: LBC Publications, 2000), p. 247.

[83] Matthew Henry, *Matthew Henry's Whole Bible Commentary*, Luke 2:40 (Sword Searcher, version 5.5.1.3) [Computer Software]. Broken Arrow, OK: StudyLamp Software LLC, 1995-2009.

[84] Herbert Lockyer, *All the Women of the Bible* (Grand Rapids, MI: Zondervan, 1967), p. 30.

[85] John MacArthur, *Grace to You*, sermon on Luke 2:36-38.

[86] *Pulpit Commentary*, Luke 20:1-2, (Sword Searcher, version 5.5.1.3) [Computer Software]. Broken Arrow, OK: StudyLamp Software LLC, 1995-2009.

[87] John G. Butler, *Jesus Christ: His Incarnation*, p. 249.

[88] Herbert Lockyer, *All the Women of the Bible* (Grand Rapids, MI: Zondervan, 1967), p. 31.

Made in United States
Orlando, FL
12 September 2022

22324207R00063